| DATE DUE | | | |
|---|---|---|---|
| | | | |
| | | | |
| | | | |
| | | | |
| | | | |
| | | | |
| | | | |
| | | | |
| | | | |
| | | | |
| | | | |
| | | | |
| | | | |

# WITH CAPTAIN JAMES COOK
# IN THE ANTARCTIC AND PACIFIC

# WITH CAPTAIN JAMES COOK IN THE ANTARCTIC AND PACIFIC

The private journal of
## James Burney
Second Lieutenant of the Adventure
on Cook's Second Voyage

*1772-1773*

Edited and with an Introduction by
BEVERLEY HOOPER

CANBERRA

NATIONAL LIBRARY OF AUSTRALIA

Burney, James, 1750–1821
  With Captain James Cook in the Antarctic and
Pacific: the private journal of James Burney,
second lieutenant of the Adventure on Cook's
second voyage, 1772–1773/edited and with an
introduction by Beverley Hooper.—Canberra:
National Library of Australia, 1975.
  Index.
  Bibliography.
  ISBN 0 642 99038 7.
  1. Cook, James, 1728–1779. 2. Pacific area—
Discovery and exploration. 3. Antarctic
regions—Discovery and exploration.
I. Hooper, Beverley, ed. II. National
Library of Australia. III. Title.

910.09164

First published in 1975 by the National Library of Australia

Copyright © 1975 by the National Library of Australia

Designed by Arthur Stokes

Maps by Gwen Bates

Printed and bound in Australia by
Brown Prior Anderson Pty Ltd, Melbourne

# PREFACE

In 1921 the distinguished collector of Australiana, Mr J. A. (later Sir John) Ferguson, purchased in London a private journal written probably for his family by James Burney, who had sailed with Captain James Cook on his second and third voyages to then unknown parts of the Antarctic, Pacific, and Arctic. The Ferguson MS, as this journal has been called, was purchased by the National Library of Australia through the good offices of Sir John's trustees, shortly after his death in 1969. The journal, of which only one extract has previously been printed, covers Cook's second voyage of 1772–5 from the departure of the sloops *Resolution* and *Adventure* from England in June 1772 until after the ships finally lost contact off New Zealand in November 1773, and the almost unseaworthy *Adventure*, in which Burney was Second Lieutenant, returned alone by Cape Horn and Cape Town to reach England in July 1774.

Burney's journal is now published by the National Library in accordance with an expressed policy of the Council that the Library should share as fully as possible with scholars, students and the general reader the original manuscripts, fascinating pictorial records, rare books, and valuable literary, historical and social material in its collections. The publication owes much to Sir Grenfell Price, CMG, who was chairman of the National Library Council at the time the journal was acquired, and who was an eager advocate of the expansion of the Library's publishing program. Happily, it is possible to illustrate the journal with some original pictures of the voyage that are in the Library's possession —a watercolour and several drawings by William Hodges, official

v

artist on board the *Resolution*; and a pencil drawing by Sir Joshua Reynolds of Omai, the young Tahitian whom Burney befriended and who sailed to England in the *Adventure*. These pictures are from the Rex Nan Kivell and Petherick collections.

G. CHANDLER
*Director-General*
*National Library of Australia*

# CONTENTS

# ILLUSTRATIONS

## MAPS

# NOTE ON THE TEXT

The text is printed exactly as Burney wrote it, except that paragraphs have been indented. The original spelling, capitalisation and punctuation have also been retained in footnote quotations from other logs and journals. Where Burney's spelling of places and persons differs from conventional usage, it is standardised in footnotes in accordance with the spelling used by J. C. Beaglehole as editor of *The Journals of Captain James Cook* for the Hakluyt Society. There are some discrepancies between the dating in Burney's private journal, written in civil time, and the dating in Cook's journal of his second voyage, written mainly in ship's (nautical) time, twelve hours ahead of civil time. Dates on maps are given in civil time to correspond with Burney's dating of events.

# INTRODUCTION

The Burney family played a prominent role in the cultural life of eighteenth- and nineteenth-century England, producing, in the words of essayist William Hazlitt, 'wits, scholars, novelists, musicians, artists, in "numbers numberless". The name alone is a passport to the Temple of Fame.'[1] Its most famous members were Dr Charles Burney, historian of music, and his daughter Fanny, novelist and diarist. Less well known, and somewhat out of place in the creative Burney circle, was James Burney, naval officer and geographer. Born in London on 13 June 1750, James was the second child and eldest son of Charles Burney, then a young church organist, and his wife Esther. Shortly after his birth, the family left London because of Charles Burney's ill health and settled at King's Lynn in Norfolk, where James had his formal education: a few terms at the local grammar school. In 1760 the Burneys returned to London but, if Charles had recovered, his wife was ailing after bearing eight children in eleven years. Her failing health was not improved by James's boisterous behaviour in the confinement of a crowded London house, and Charles Burney decided that his son, almost ten years old, should go to sea.[2]

---

[1] William Hazlitt, 'On the Aristocracy of Letters', in A. R. Waller and Arnold Glover (ed.), *The Collected Works of William Hazlitt* (13 vols, London, 1902–6), Vol. VI, p. 209.

[2] The factual details of James Burney's life are based on G. E. Manwaring, *My Friend the Admiral. The Life, Letters, and Journals of Rear-Admiral James Burney, F.R.S. The Companion of Captain Cook and Friend of Charles Lamb* (London, 1931); article on James Burney in *Dictionary of National Biography* (London, 1886), Vol. VII, p. 419; and works on other members of the Burney family,

It was not unusual for boys to join the Royal Navy at such an early age. One way of preparing to become a naval officer was to undergo two years' training at the Royal Naval Academy at Portsmouth, for which the minimum age of entry was twelve. A more popular method was to obtain an appointment as 'captain's servant' and receive practical training in seamanship. In mid 1760, shortly after his tenth birthday, James Burney was appointed captain's servant in the *Princess Amelia*, serving in the Bay of Biscay and later off Brest. Two years later he was transferred with his captain to the *Magnanime*. With Britain involved in the Seven Years War against France, young James found life at sea far more adventurous than doing school work or teaching his favourite younger sister, Fanny, to read. When peace was declared in 1763 the excitement declined but James continued his training, serving as captain's servant and later as midshipman in Royal Navy ships in the Mediterranean area. He ventured farther afield in 1770 when he followed the peacetime example of many other young naval trainees by serving in an East India Company ship on a return voyage to Bombay. James arrived back in England in May 1771. Not quite twenty-one, he was already an experienced sailor.

Two months later, James Cook returned to England in the *Endeavour* after his successful first voyage. It was the age of Pacific exploration, the chief drawcard being *Terra Australis*—the mythical southern continent. In the sixteenth century, Spanish expeditions—led by Magellan, Mendana and de Quiros—had visited the Pacific in search of spices, gold and converts to Christianity. In the seventeenth and early eighteenth centuries Dutch voyagers, including Tasman, Hartog, Schouten, le Maire and Roggeveen, sailed to the East Indies and the Pacific in search of trade. By the second half of the eighteenth century England and France had taken the initiative in Pacific exploration, combining their interest in geographical research with their continued imperial rivalry after the Seven Years War. The British explorers Byron, Carteret and Wallis, and the Frenchman de Bougainville,

---

including: Madame d'Arblay, *Memoirs of Doctor Burney* (3 vols, London, 1832); Charlotte Barrett (ed.), *Diary and Letters of Madame d'Arblay, 1778–1840* (6 vols, London, 1904–5); Annie Raine Ellis (ed.), *The Early Diary of Frances Burney 1768–1778* (2 vols, London, 1907); Joyce Hemlow, *The History of Fanny Burney* (Oxford, 1958); R. Brimley Johnson, *Fanny Burney and the Burneys* (London, 1926); and Percy Scholes, *The Great Doctor Burney* (2 vols, London, 1948).

followed routes across the Pacific fairly similar to those of earlier explorers.

Stormy weather in the southern temperate zone, together with the need for repairs and supplies, had forced Cook's predecessors northward to the Pacific Islands, leaving the eastern Pacific unexplored in latitudes beyond 30°S and the western Pacific beyond 20°S. There might still be a great southern continent south of these latitudes between New Zealand and South America. In August 1768 Cook left for the Pacific to observe the transit of Venus and to search for the southern continent. After spending three months at Tahiti, he sailed to New Zealand, which he circumnavigated, and then west until he reached the Australian continent. By the end of the voyage he had not only defined Australia's eastern coastline; he had also established that any continent between New Zealand and South America had to be beyond 40°S.[1]

The British Government decided to send Cook on a second voyage to the Pacific to settle, once and for all, whether or not there was a southern continent. When James Burney heard about the proposed voyage, he told his father he wanted to take part in it. Patronage did the rest. Dr Charles Burney was now a prominent figure in London's musical and social world. More importantly for James, he was a close friend of Lord Sandwich, First Lord of the Admiralty, dispenser of favours and, amongst less cultured pursuits, lover of music. When Dr Burney approached Lord Sandwich on James's behalf, Sandwich invited father and son to his country residence to meet Captain Cook and Sir Joseph Banks. The meeting had the desired result. In December 1771, James Burney was appointed able seaman in Cook's ship the *Resolution*, preparing to sail for the Pacific with the *Adventure*, under the command of Tobias Furneaux.[2]

It is part of Cook's second voyage that James Burney describes in the private journal printed in this volume. The *Resolution*, accompanied by the *Adventure*, left England in June 1772. On 18 November, while the ships were at the Cape of Good Hope, Burney was transferred to the *Adventure* as second lieutenant

---

[1] The history of Pacific exploration and the search for the southern continent are summarised by J. C. Beaglehole, *The Exploration of the Pacific*, third ed. (London, 1966).

[2] d'Arblay, *Memoirs of Doctor Burney*, Vol. I, pp. 269–70.

in one of a number of moves resulting from the departure of the *Adventure's* first lieutenant, Joseph Shank, who returned to England because of ill health. Although Burney had passed his lieutenant's certificate over a year earlier after turning twenty-one, he had been appointed to the *Adventure* as only able seaman—with the promise of promotion as soon as a vacancy occurred. Cook found Burney 'very deserving'; Burney now had his first commission.[1]

After leaving the Cape of Good Hope, the ships proceeded south. Cook had instructions to find Cape Circumcision, sighted in the South Atlantic half a century earlier by Lozier Bouvet who thought he had discovered the southern continent. If he did not find the cape, Cook was to sail south until he reached a solid land mass—hopefully the elusive continent—and then circumnavigate the globe, in as high a latitude as necessary, keeping in contact with the land. The ships failed to locate the cape and continued south, crossing the Antarctic Circle for the first time in history. With the summer season well advanced, no land in sight and the *Resolution* and *Adventure* surrounded by pack ice, Cook decided to go no farther. Soon after changing course, the ships lost contact in the fog. Both sailed to New Zealand. On the way, the *Adventure* made the first British visit to Tasmania, with Burney leading the first expedition ashore.

After meeting up at Queen Charlotte Sound in New Zealand, the two ships spent the southern winter on an exploratory cruise to the Society Islands and Tonga, separating again on the return voyage to New Zealand when the *Adventure* had difficulty entering Cook Strait. By the time she reached Queen Charlotte Sound, Cook had left on his second trip to the Antarctic. Soon afterwards, Burney had his most devastating experience of the voyage when he led an expedition to nearby Grass Cove in search of ten of the *Adventure's* men, finding only the remains of a Maori cannibal feast. With the *Adventure* crank and leaking, Furneaux soon decided against any further exploration and returned to England. James Burney's first voyage round the world—the most exciting period of his life to date—was over. Cook himself made two further trips to the Antarctic, completing the circumnavigation of the

---

[1] Cook to Burney, 18 November 1772. Enc. in Cook to Stephens, 18 November 1772. *Historical Records of New South Wales*, I, i, pp. 371–2; d'Arblay, *Memoirs of Doctor Burney*, Vol. I, p. 271.

globe, and another winter cruise to the Pacific Islands. When he arrived back in England in July 1775, a year after the *Adventure*, his charts demonstrated convincingly that there was no southern continent. The search was over.[1]

On his return to England, Burney had not only a private journal to show his family and friends but also a South Sea Islander. Omai, a native of the Society Islands, had sailed to England as a passenger in the *Adventure*. Burney was about the same age as Omai and befriended the young man on the homeward voyage, not so much to make him feel at home in such strange company as to find out more about the Society Islands and their inhabitants, whose way of life had fascinated him. If Omai made little progress in learning English, Burney quickly picked up the rudiments of Omai's native language and was in demand as an interpreter when the South Sea Islander made his debut on the London scene. Omai was a great success in England. He was presented at Court, enjoyed the patronage of Lord Sandwich, Sir Joseph Banks and Dr Solander, and became the darling of London's society ladies, who saw him as the live representation of the Rousseauian 'noble savage'. When he dined with the Burneys, Fanny found him so graceful and attentive that he could well have come 'from some foreign Court'. She was no less impressed with her brother's apparent command of Omai's native language: 'You cannot suppose how fluently and easily Jem speaks it.'[2]

While Omai was making his presence felt in London, Burney was switching his thoughts from Pacific adventure to imperialism and rebellion in Britain's American colonies. In December 1774, just one year after the Boston Tea Party, he was appointed second lieutenant of the *Cerberus*, a fast Royal Navy frigate charged with the task of transporting three major-generals and British troops to America to assist General Gage, Governor of Massachusetts. On 18 April 1775, two days before the *Cerberus*

[1] The major source for Cook's second voyage is J. C. Beaglehole (ed.) *The Journals of Captain James Cook on his Voyages of Discovery, II, The Voyage of the Resolution and Adventure, 1772–1775* (Cambridge, 1961). For Furneaux's accounts of the *Adventure's* voyage when separated from the *Resolution*, see PRO Adm. 55/1 and B.M. Add. MS. 27890. Extracts of these journals are printed in Beaglehole, *Cook Journals*, II, pp. 143–60, 729–45.

[2] Fanny Burney to Samuel Crisp, 1 December 1774, in Ellis, *Early Diary of Frances Burney*, Vol. I, pp. 333–4. See also T. B. Clark, *Omai, First Polynesian Ambassador to England* (San Francisco, 1941), and *Omiah's Farewell: Inscribed to the Ladies of London* (London, 1776).

left England, the first shots of the conflict were fired at Lexington. The *Cerberus* carried out her mission, returned to England, and a few weeks later made a second trip across the Atlantic with medical supplies and a detachment of marines. On the ship's arrival at Boston, Burney received news of his reward for his efficient performance on board the *Adventure*: promotion to first lieutenant. Despite his new rank, trips across the Atlantic seemed very routine compared with the excitement of voyaging round the world with Cook. Three weeks later, when the *Cerberus* returned to Boston after patrolling the Massachusetts coastline, memories of those fascinating far-off places became vivid in Burney's mind. Before leaving England, he had told his father he was keen to sail on a proposed third voyage to the Pacific. Dr Burney again used his influence with Lord Sandwich, who subsequently requested that James be permitted to return to England if he wished to accompany Cook. With no qualms about leaving the *Cerberus*, he sailed for England in the first available ship.[1]

The aim of Cook's third voyage—apart from returning Omai to his native land—was to discover the North-West Passage. For almost three hundred years men had been searching for an ice-free route linking the Atlantic to the Pacific, and in 1745 the British Government offered a reward of £20,000 for the discovery of such a passage. Cook again commanded the *Resolution* and Burney was appointed first lieutenant of the *Discovery*, captained by Charles Clerke. When Clerke was delayed in London with financial problems, Burney had his first taste of command, sailing the *Discovery* from the Thames to Plymouth. Fanny Burney, always ambitious for her favourite brother, wrote excitedly to a close family friend, Samuel Crisp, that 'Jem' was 'now, in *fact* and in *power*, Captain of his ship, though, alas! not in *honour* or *profit*'.[2] The triumph was short-lived. Clerke eventually joined the *Discovery* and she left Plymouth on 1 August 1776, three weeks after the *Resolution*. The two ships met at the Cape of Good Hope, sailed south to explore Kerguelen Island, and then on to Tasmania,

---

[1] Fanny Burney to Samuel Crisp, 14 April 1775, in Ellis, *Early Diary of Frances Burney*, Vol. II, p. 38; James Burney, *A Chronological History of North-Eastern Voyages of Discovery; and of the early Eastern navigations of the Russians* (London, 1819), p. 202.

[2] Fanny Burney to Samuel Crisp, July 1776, in Ellis, *Early Diary of Frances Burney*, Vol. II, p. 140.

New Zealand, Tonga and the Society Islands. All this was familiar territory to Burney and his superiors. The voyagers broke new ground in January 1777 when they became the first known Europeans to visit Hawaii. During the summer they explored the coast of Alaska, venturing north of the Bering Strait and the Arctic Circle, but were unable to find a passage to the Atlantic.

After failing to find the North-West Passage, Cook decided to spend the northern winter at Hawaii—a fatal decision. The natives were initially friendly and treated the Europeans to lavish ceremonies, but, like most Pacific Islanders, they rewarded their own generosity by thieving all they could from their visitors. The climax came when the *Discovery's* cutter was stolen on the night of 13–14 February 1779. What followed has become legend. Cook, Lieutenant Molesworth Phillips and nine marines went ashore and took a local chief hostage for the cutter. When they were about to return to the ships they were attacked on the beach by a crowd of natives. Cook and four marines were killed. Of all the accounts of Cook's death, Burney's journal report was one of the most concise and unemotional. Burney was not a man without feelings and was probably no less affected by Cook's murder than were other witnesses; yet he always believed that colourful language and the expression of personal emotions only distorted the record. Facts came first; feelings were a private matter for the individual. Burney himself went ashore later in the day when he and Second Lieutenant James King braved a tense situation in an unsuccessful attempt to persuade the natives to hand over the bodies of Cook and the four murdered marines. Parts of Cook's body and his bones were later returned to the *Resolution*.[1]

With Cook dead, Charles Clerke took command and in the following summer the ships returned north to make another futile search for the North-West Passage. Clerke himself died in August 1779, only six months after Cook. Burney was transferred to the *Resolution*, retaining his rank of first lieutenant, for the

[1] James Burney, *Journal* (Mitchell Library Manuscript). Burney's journal entries for 6–14 February are printed as 'The Last Days of Captain Cook' in A. Grove Day and Carl Stroven (ed.), *A Hawaiian Reader* (New York, 1959), pp. 11–19. Cf. Burney's account with descriptions by surgeon David Samwell, *Narrative of the Death of Captain James Cook* (London, 1786), and Commander Charles Clerke, in J. C. Beaglehole (ed.), *The Journals of Captain James Cook on his Voyages of Discovery*, III, *The Voyage of the Resolution and Discovery 1776–1780* (Cambridge, 1967), pp. 533–40.

homeward voyage via Macao and the Cape of Good Hope. Circumstances had put him in command of the *Discovery* for a few weeks before he left England; they did the same again for the last few weeks of the voyage. After the ships' arrival in the Orkneys in August 1780, James King, who had captained the *Discovery* on her passage back to England, left for London to report to the Admiralty. Burney went back to the *Discovery* and, even though he was the fourth officer to command the ship in the one voyage, the Admiralty commissioned him as commander on 2 October, two days before the ships arrived back in the Thames. Promotion was virtually automatic for those who survived.[1]

After an absence of over four years, James Burney was welcomed back into the Burney family, a family that was becoming increasingly prominent with the reputation of Dr Charles Burney being challenged by that of his daughter, Fanny, whose first novel *Evelina* had been published two years earlier. The Burney circle encompassed a wide range of literary and social celebrities, including Dr Samuel Johnson and Mrs Thrale's Streatham group. The presence of sailor James, now a mature man of thirty, added a touch of adventure to their gatherings. His latest stories, told with good humour and much gusto, made him a welcome and entertaining guest, even if his appearance and manner appeared somewhat incongruous in such company. A rather squat figure, his face already bore the weather-beaten mark of years of exposure to the elements. It was not improved by a long nose, a prominent lower lip, bushy eyebrows and unruly hair. Nor did James have the refinements normally expected of an English gentleman: he dressed carelessly; he was honest to the point of being embarrassingly blunt; his stories were not always suitable for female ears. But this could be excused of a man who had spent most of his life at sea, and, even if he did appear boisterous and uncultured on the surface, his friends recognised his underlying warmth and amiability. Dr Johnson was surprised, indeed, that Burney was so 'gentle in his manners etc., tho' he had lived so many years with sailors and savages'.[2]

---

[1] For details of Cook's third voyage and the journals of other officers, see Beaglehole, *Cook Journals*, III. Cook's third voyage, together with earlier attempts to find the North-West Passage, were described forty years after the voyage by Burney, *Chronological History of North-Eastern Voyages of Discovery*.

[2] Mrs Thrale to Fanny Burney, 22 December 1780, in Barrett, *Diary and Letters of Madame d'Arblay*, Vol. I, p. 454; Ellis, *Early Diary of Frances Burney*, Vol. I, pp. 67–8.

Welcome though he was, James was not keen to spend more than a few months with his family and friends. A practical man of action, he was quite happy to give up the comforts of life ashore for the rigours of life at sea. More important was his ambition for the success and recognition already enjoyed by his father and sister. He had already had his first taste of command: soon he should have his own ship. First, in November 1781, came a temporary appointment as captain of the *Latona*, a thirty-eight gun frigate, during the absence of the ship's usual captain. Temporary or not, the news of the appointment was enough to make him, in the excited words of Fanny Burney, 'almost frantic with ecstasy of joy; he sang, laughed, drank to his own success, and danced about the room'.[1] Dr Johnson expressed his congratulations in a more solemn tone when he wrote: 'I question if any ship upon the ocean goes out attended with more good wishes than that which carries the fate of Burney'.[2] The enthusiasm was somewhat premature. In March 1782, after an uneventful three-month cruise in the North Sea, Burney was relieved of his command.

Three months later Burney achieved his immediate ambition when he was commissioned as post-captain in the Royal Navy. His ship was the fifty-gun *Bristol* and his destination India, where fresh hostilities had broken out between England and France. Twelve years earlier Burney had sailed to India as an ordinary seaman in an East Indiaman; now his own ship had the task of convoying twelve East India Company ships and two armed store ships to Madras. The *Bristol* arrived off Madras in April 1783 and joined Sir Edward Hughes's squadron. Hughes had already fought four engagements with the French fleet under the colourful Admiral Suffren, and on 20 June the *Bristol* participated in the fifth and final engagement off Cuddalore. When the battle was over, she had ten men wounded, damaged masts and rigging, and several holes in the hull. The honours of the day went to the French, who anchored off Cuddalore while the British fleet retired to Madras; the participants did not know that the British

---

[1] Fanny Burney to Mrs Thrale. The date on the letter is 4 November 1780 but it must have been written a year later as Burney did not receive news of his appointment until 2 November 1781. Barrett, *Diary and Letters of Madame d'Arblay*, Vol. I, p. 453.

[2] Samuel Johnson to Mrs Thrale, 14 November 1781, in R. W. Chapman (ed.), *The Letters of Samuel Johnson* (3 vols., Oxford, 1952), Vol. II, letter no. 749.

and French governments had signed a peace treaty five months earlier.

After the battle against the French, the remaining eighteen months that Burney spent with the *Bristol* cruising in Indian waters seemed an anti-climax. Although he was normally a healthy man and had not suffered seriously from scurvy or dysentery on his two voyages with Cook, he now fell victim to the Indian climate and by the end of 1784 was seriously ill. Doctors who examined him at the Naval Hospital in Bombay diagnosed a chronic liver obstruction and stated that he could not expect to recover in India. Late in December he sailed for England on board the *Europa*, one of the ships he had convoyed to India. Little did Burney know that this was to be his last long sea voyage. He had been at sea almost continuously since the age of ten during an exciting period of exploration and European rivalry. Now, at thirty-four, his active naval career was over.

When Burney arrived back in England in July 1785 after a sea voyage of over six months, Fanny reported that her brother had recovered and was now 'very well'.[1] Less then two months later he married Sally Payne, whom he had courted during his last two periods ashore. Sally, now in her late twenties, was the younger and plainer daughter of Thomas Payne, proprietor of the famous L-shaped bookshop next to the Mews Gate in London which was frequented by the leading literary men of the day. After his marriage, Burney bought a small property at Mickleham in Surrey, near the home of his sister Susan and her husband Molesworth Phillips, who had also sailed on Cook's third voyage. In 1792, on the death of John Hayes, an old family friend who was reputed to be the natural son of Sir Robert Walpole, Burney inherited a London residence in fashionable James Street, Westminster. The Burney couple moved into the house with their four-year-old son, Martin. In 1796 a daughter, Sally, was born. A second daughter, Katherine, died in infancy.

Although Burney's domestic life was initially contented, he was anxious to resume his naval career. Unfortunately for ambitious officers, England was now at peace and her reduced naval strength meant that most captains were ashore on half-pay. James Burney was no exception. When his own attempts to obtain another

[1] Fanny Burney to Miss Thrale, 28 July 1785, in H. H. Keith (ed.), *The Queeney Letters* (London, 1934), p. 111.

commission were unsuccessful, he hoped family influence would again come to his aid. Fanny now held a position at Court and made a direct, if flippant, approach to the Queen on her brother's behalf in 1790. Nothing came of it.[1] More puzzling was Burney's failure to obtain a commission after war broke out with France in 1793. Certainly, his early progress in the Royal Navy had been due largely to the patronage of Lord Sandwich, whose own career as First Lord of the Admiralty had ended abruptly in 1782. As for his own merits, Burney had failed to make a reputation as an outstanding naval officer. But nor had he made any disastrous blunders. Well trained and capable, his straightforward manner and fairmindedness earned him the respect of his subordinates. According to James Trevenen, a young midshipman on Cook's third voyage, Burney was 'not only a good man, but a good seaman, [and] a good officer'.[2] His attitude to ordinary seamen was, perhaps, a little too easy-going and humane to make him a great leader in a profession which demanded strong discipline and absolute obedience to authority.[3] But probably his major failing, so far as his superiors were concerned, was his openly expressed sympathy for democratic principles at a time when Pitt's government was fighting against the revolutionary cause. Dr Burney, who had done all in his power to further his son's early naval career, attributed James's loss of favour at the Admiralty purely and simply to his political beliefs.[4]

Burney eventually realised that his naval ambitions had been thwarted but he had no intention of following the lead of those half-pay officers who retired to the country and spent the rest of their lives hunting and reliving their experiences at sea. He must find a new road to success if he was to have any chance of keeping abreast of his famous family. Dr Charles Burney was now an established musical historian whose publications included a four-volume *History of Music* and writings on his European travels. James's only brother, Charles, was becoming well known as a classical critic and editor of the *London Magazine*. Fanny had

---

[1] Barrett, *Diary and Letters of Madame d'Arblay*, Vol. IV, p. 376, entry for 10 May 1790.
[2] James Trevenen to his mother, 9 September 1780, in Christopher Lloyd and R. C. Anderson (ed.), *A Memoir of James Trevenen* (London, 1959), p. 35.
[3] This is suggested in Burney's obituary in *The Times*, 20 November 1821.
[4] Charles Burney to Charles Burney Jnr, 31 May 1808, quoted by Hemlow, *The History of Fanny Burney*, pp. 425–6.

become the most famous Burney of all when her novels made her a celebrated literary figure. Other Burneys were making their reputations as artists and harpsichordists.

Despite James's lack of formal education, he was not overawed for long in this company. First, he decided to make up the ground he had lost—but not in the usual Burney world of literature, music and the arts in general. James was no dilettante but a practical man of the world; while other young Englishman had been completing their cultural education on the Grand Tour of France and Italy, James had been doing his own rigorous Grand Tour of the Pacific, the Antarctic and the Arctic. So when he ventured into academic study, he concentrated on practical subjects. Shortly after his return to England, his sister Susan told Fanny that James was busy studying 'all kinds of things at once—Law—Physics—Politics—and History—besides French, and Latin'. Accustomed to years of routine, he set himself the goal of reading one hundred pages a day until he had acquired the requisite knowledge.[1]

The requisite knowledge for what? Preferring action to contemplation, Burney decide to put his newly acquired knowledge to practical use and turned to writing—like his father, brother and sister before him. But he received no credit for his first effort, a contribution to a work in which his involvement has only recently been proved. In consultation with Sir Joseph Banks, he spent the latter part of 1791 compiling the narrative, based on William Bligh's journal, of the *Bounty's* fatal voyage to Tahiti in 1788–9. Bligh, who had become friendly with Burney on Cook's third voyage, had left for the Pacific to make a second attempt to transfer the breadfruit from Tahiti to the West Indies. In 1792 Burney saw the book through the press. Burney's own contribution included the addition of remarks, for a long time attributed to Bligh himself, on the merits of emigration from over-populated Tahiti to under-populated New Holland, colonised four years earlier by Governor Phillip. According to Burney, New Holland was 'as if designed by nature to serve as an asylum for the super-flux of inhabitants in the islands'. Not only would 'a great continent . . . be converted from a desert to a populous country [but] a number of our fellow-creatures would be saved'. It was

---

[1] Susan Burney to Fanny Burney, 25 March 1787. Printed in Johnson, *Fanny Burney and the Burneys*, p. 126.

not improbable, indeed, that the 'colonies in New Holland would derive so much benefit as to more than repay any trouble of expence [sic], that might be incurred in endeavouring to promote so humane a plan'.[1]

Next, Burney tried his hand at short works on contemporary affairs, a special interest after spending so long out of touch with day-to-day political events. In 1797 he published two pamphlets. The first, prompted by the threatened French invasion of Ireland, was entitled *Plan of Defence Against Invasion* and suggested that all male civilians receive basic military training so that an army could be called out at a moment's notice. Later the same year, in *Measures Recommended for the Support of Public Credit*, he put forward a number of suggestions on how to combat the current monetary crisis, brought about when the threat of invasion caused a run on the Bank of England. The pamphlets were reviewed in the *Monthly Review* and aroused widespread interest, if not wide acclaim.[2]

Burney's new career was interrupted by a crisis in his private life. His marriage did not live up to its early hopes and his eye began to wander; unfortunately it wandered only as far as his half-sister, Sarah Harriet, the daughter of Charles Burney and his second wife, whom he married after the death of James's mother. Sarah Harriet had grown up in the shadow of her famous relatives, who considered her plain and sullen, her only redeeming physical feature being her luxuriant hair. When the Burney family saw James spending less time at home with his wife and children, and more time with Sarah Harriet, they became suspicious and anxious. Their worst fears were realised in September 1798 when the pair eloped. James was forty-eight; Sarah Harriet twenty-six.

---

[1] Manwaring, *My Friend the Admiral*, pp. 198–201, suspected, but had no positive evidence, that Burney was involved in the publication of William Bligh's *A Voyage to the South Sea in H.M.S. Bounty; including an account of the mutiny on board the said ship* (London, 1792). Burney's role is apparent from three letters he wrote to Sir Joseph Banks on 5 September, 13 October and 22 October 1791, which are discussed by Rolf du Rietz, 'Three Letters from James Burney to Sir Joseph Banks. A Contribution to the History of William Bligh's "A Voyage to the South Sea" ', *Ethnos*, 27 (1962), pp. 115–25. In the second and third of the letters, Burney suggested adding 'some reflections' on Tahitian society, including his emigration plan, the wording being virtually identical to that in Bligh's published narrative. For the relevant passages, see Bligh, *A Voyage to the South Sea*, pp. 80–1, and letters from Burney to Banks of 13 and 22 October 1791, printed in du Rietz, *Ethnos*, 27, pp. 122–4.

[2] *Monthly Review*, 22 (1797), pp. 338–9, 465–6.

Fanny Burney could scarcely believe that her dear, honest brother was capable of 'leading another astray' and dreaded the thought of meeting him eye to eye. Dr Burney, now seventy-two years old, was horrified and angered at the scandalous behaviour of his two offspring and declared he would never again live under the same roof with such people. In spite of their shock, the Burneys closed ranks and did their best to hide the truth from others. James, they said, had separated from his wife and Sarah Harriet was keeping house for him.[1]

James and Sarah Harriet spent five years together, moving from London to Bristol and later back to London. When the affair broke up, they were duly taken back into the family fold as the prodigal son and daughter. James returned to his all-forgiving wife and absorbed himself in writing. Dr Burney's relations with his son were never quite the same again but he eventually forgave Sarah Harriet and she returned to Chelsea to care for him and to resume her own career as a novelist. She did not marry. Fanny Burney had at last accepted that her brother was not perfect and that his humane interest in society at large did not always extend to the members of his own family. Close as James was to his father and sisters, he had shown no more concern for their feelings than for conventional social norms: he made his own rules, in his private as in his professional life. Fanny later maintained that, throughout his life, James had the 'excentric idea he might hold himself above the controul of opinion, or custom [sic]'.[2]

While he was living with his half-sister, Burney decided to embark on the large-scale work which he hoped would make him famous. He was over fifty: the time was past for fiddling with trifles. As one of the few surviving officers of Cook's voyages, there was one subject on which he could claim to be as knowledgeable as almost anyone else: Pacific exploration. He had spent the most exciting years of his life sailing round the world with Cook;

---

[1] Burney's biographer, Manwaring, gave no indication of Burney's domestic problems and Scholes, *The Great Doctor Burney*, Vol. II, p. 232, stated that Burney 'seems to have been very happy' with his wife. The details of Burney's relationship with his half-sister, Sarah Harriet, are based on a number of letters from Maria Allen Rishton to Fanny Burney, Fanny Burney to Captain Molesworth Phillips, and Charles Burney to Fanny Burney, quoted by Hemlow, *The History of Fanny Burney*, pp. 281–5.

[2] Fanny Burney to Esther Burney, 23 November 1821, quoted by Hemlow, *The History of Fanny Burney*, p. 429.

now he would write a history of Cook's predecessors in the South
Pacific. The work was an ambitious one. Entitled *A Chronological
History of the Discoveries in the South Sea or Pacific Ocean*, it was
published in five volumes, the first appearing in 1803 and the
fifth in 1817. Probably the most popular section was the part
of Volume IV entitled *History of the Buccaneers of America*, printed
also as a separate edition.[1] Even though Burney's five-volume
history was a major undertaking in itself, he intended it as part of
a broader project. He explained in the preface to the first volume,
dedicated to his friend and guide, Sir Joseph Banks, that he was
contributing to what he hoped would be a complete 'Digest of
Maritime Geographical Discovery', a work which had 'long been
wanted'.[2]

Burney's own volumes traced the history of Pacific exploration
from Magellan's voyage in the early sixteenth century to Bougainville's in the mid eighteenth, stopping short of Cook. According to
Burney, the main fault of many previous collections of travels
was their carelessness of arrangement. His own study reflected a
systematic approach: he was a thorough researcher, drawing
on the journals of the voyagers themselves and earlier historians;
he arranged his material in an orderly fashion and presented it
in concise, crisp prose; he gave each volume a comprehensive
table of contents, several charts and explanatory footnotes.
Burney had done a professional piece of work and his industry
was well rewarded. The first volume was praised as 'a very
valuable addition to our maritime history' and subsequent
volumes were equally well received.[3] Burney had, indeed, produced the standard work on exploration in the South Pacific.
Spurred on by his success, he embarked on a supplementary one-
volume history of the search for a northern passage linking
Europe to Asia, including Cook's third voyage on which he
himself had sailed, as well as Russian exploration along the
country's northern and eastern coastlines. Published in 1819
when Burney was sixty-nine years old, the volume was entitled
*A Chronological History of North-Eastern Voyages of Discovery; and of*

---

[1] James Burney, *History of the Buccaneers of America*, London, 1816. Subsequent reprintings included London, 1891, 1907, 1949, and New York, 1902.
[2] James Burney, *A Chronological History of the Discoveries in the South Sea or
Pacific Ocean* (5 vols., London, 1803–17), Vol. I, p. i.
[3] *Annual Review and History of Literature*, Vol. 2, 1803, pp. 3–12; *Quarterly
Review*, Vol. 17, 1817, pp. 1–39.

*the early Eastern navigations of the Russians.* This was Burney's last major work. His histories of exploration had finally given him the personal fame he had long sought and added his name to the literary reputation of the Burney family.

Like many prominent men of his time, Burney also made occasional digressions into the learned world of the Royal Society, currently presided over by Sir Joseph Banks. In 1809 he read two papers to the Society: *Observations on the Progress of Bodies Floating in a Stream* and *New Method Proposed for Measuring a Ship's Rate of Sailing.* Both proved too technical to receive the approval of those present. Later the same year, Burney was elected a Fellow of the Royal Society, not so much for his papers as in recognition of the two volumes of his history which had so far been published. Satisfied that he had finally gained recognition but angered by the poor reception his scientific papers had received, he did not bother to complete the formalities and become a member of the Society until 1815. A further paper and two pamphlets completed his writings on scientific and geographical subjects.[1]

If Burney spent most of his days alone at his writing desk, he spent most of his evenings with friends playing whist, one of the card games that had swept England in the mid eighteenth century. Burney's newly won fame, as well as his family, brought him into contact with well-known literary figures who also enjoyed the game—men like essayists Charles Lamb and William Hazlitt, diarist Henry Crabb Robinson, and poet Robert Southey. These men belonged to the so-called 'Lamb Circle' that met regularly to play whist, especially at Lamb's 'Wednesday evenings' which became something of an institution. Lamb's guests, wrote Crabb Robinson, were 'a numerous and odd set ... for the greater part interesting and amusing people'.[2] Burney took his whist seriously and thought others should do the same, as Crabb

---

[1] In December 1817 Burney read a paper to the Royal Society, published the following year as *A Memoir on the Geography of the North-Eastern Part of Asia, and on the question whether Asia and America are contiguous, or are separated by the sea.* In 1819 he published a pamphlet entitled *A Commentary on the Systems which have been advanced for explaining the Planetary Motions* and in 1820 *A Memoir on the Voyage of d'Entrecasteaux, in search of La Pérouse.*

[2] Thomas Sadler (ed.), *Diary, Reminiscences, and Correspondence of Henry Crabb Robinson* (3 vols., London, 1869), Vol. I, p. 487. See also *ibid.*, p. 300. The whist parties at Lamb's and Burney's are described also by Barry Cornwall, *Charles Lamb: A Memoir* (London, 1869), pp. 126–7, 140–6, and William Hazlitt, 'On the Conversation of Authors', in Waller and Glover, *The Collected Works of William Hazlitt*, Vol. VII, pp. 35–8.

Robinson found out when he was soundly scolded by Burney for playing badly.[1] Keen as ever to demonstrate his supremacy, Burney treated the game as a new challenge and soon considered himself an authority on the subject. So much so, in fact, that in 1821 he published what was to be his last pamphlet, *An Essay, by way of Lecture, on the Game of Whist*, in which he warned his readers that good play could not be achieved without long practice and earnest attention. It was a serious business.[2]

Yet Burney was a sociable man and he enjoyed sharing stories and jokes with his companions—at least when there was a break in the game for a supper of cold beef or lamb, roast potatoes and porter. Even though he had spent longer ashore than at sea, his friends still regarded him as the 'old captain': the humorous, talkative old sailor who had twice sailed round the world with Captain Cook and who still had entertaining stories to tell about those adventurous days and about the foibles of human nature. 'A merry *natural* captain,' wrote Charles Lamb after their first meeting.[3] Burney's many years in polite society had neither corrupted his basic honesty nor polished his rough edges. He was, said Crabb Robinson, indeed 'a character, a fine, noble creature—gentle, with a rough exterior'.[4] He still had no time for social affectation; he still told yarns which made his sisters blush; and he took no more interest in his appearance than he had done as a young man. In 1821, when Charles Lamb attended the wedding of Burney's daughter, Sally, he was astonished to find his friend 'in fine wig and buckle . . . a striking contrast to his usual neglect of personal appearance'.[5]

Burney himself was a genial and informal host, entertaining his guests with 'flashes of wild wit' in a disorderly household where chairs and candles were scattered at random, where tea and supper were likely to be served at once, and where host and guest conversed on different topics with neither listening to the other.

[1] Sadler, *Diary, Reminiscences and Correspondence of Henry Crabb Robinson*, Vol. I, p. 476.

[2] James Burney, *An Essay, by way of Lecture, on the Game of Whist* (London, 1821). Part of the essay is reprinted in Johnson, *Fanny Burney and the Burneys*, pp. 338–43.

[3] Lamb to Manning, 19 February 1803, in A. Ainger (ed.), *The Letters of Charles Lamb* (2 vols, London, 1904), Vol. I, p. 244.

[4] Sadler, *Diary, Reminiscences, and Correspondence of Henry Crabb Robinson*, Vol. I, p. 300.

[5] Charles Lamb, 'The Wedding', *The Essays of Elia* (London, 1883), p. 319.

Lamb knew of no other house in London where harmony was 'so strangely the result of confusion'.[1] Few realised that beneath Burney's easy-going nature there was a deep sensitivity and a protective instinct towards members of his family which persisted despite his own disregard for their feelings. In February 1815, Burney's card-playing companion, William Hazlitt, wrote a scathing review of Fanny Burney's novel *The Wanderer*. Burney took this as a personal attack, not only on his sister but on the literary reputation of the entire Burney family, and informed Hazlitt in writing that their friendship was terminated.[2]

It was in his relations with the Admiralty that Burney's easily hurt pride became most apparent. In 1804 he became eligible for promotion to flag rank, having finally reached the top of the Captains' List, which was based on seniority. Because of the small number of flag positions, most captains due for promotion were placed on the retired list, normally with the lowest flag rank, that of rear-admiral. Despite Burney's growing literary reputation— the first volume of his history of Pacific exploration had been published in the previous year—his democratic tendencies were still unpopular with the Admiralty and he was placed on the retired list without promotion. If he was angry then, he was furious two years later when the Admiralty rejected his petition to George III requesting that he be admitted to flag rank. Although it was over twenty years since Burney had been to sea, he had never stopped thinking of himself as an officer of the Royal Navy. As he grew older, he became more and more outspoken in his criticism of the Admiralty's fickle ways and more and more obsessed with obtaining the recognition to which he felt entitled. It was not until July 1821 that Burney was finally promoted to the rank of rear-admiral on the retired list, and then only because of the assistance of the Duke of Clarence, Admiral of the Fleet. Patronage—and the lack of it—had guided Burney's naval career from start to finish.

Promotion had come just in time. Four months later, on 17 November 1821, at the age of seventy-one, Burney died after a stroke and was buried in the churchyard of St Margaret's,

[1] Charles Lamb, 'The Wedding', *The Essays of Elia*, pp. 320–1.
[2] James Burney to William Hazlitt, 17 May 1815. Printed in Manwaring, *My Friend the Admiral*, p. 250.

Westminster.[1] His friends mourned him as a lost card-playing companion. 'There's Captain Burney gone! What fun has whist now?' wrote Charles Lamb to William Wordsworth.[2] His press obituary mentioned his voyages with Captain Cook and his humanity as a naval officer, but not his capabilities in that profession. It reserved its praise for his later role in life as 'one of the most scientific and best geographers that this country has produced'.[3] Rear-Admiral James Burney, F.R.S., had made his name for posterity, but not in the profession in which he had most wanted to succeed.

JAMES BURNEY'S
PRIVATE JOURNAL

James Burney's fame as a writer was still a long way in the future when, as a young man of twenty-two, he sailed on Cook's second voyage. From the date of his appointment as second lieutenant of the *Adventure* in November 1772, he kept his first official log and journal.[4] On the same voyage, Burney also wrote a private journal which was less formal and more detailed than his official writings.[5] This was probably intended for his family and friends, most of whom were enthusiastic letter-writers and journal-keepers. The private journal covers the period from 22 June 1772, when Burney left England in the *Resolution*, to 22 December 1773, when the *Adventure*, having lost contact with the *Resolution*, left New Zealand to return to England.

Burney's private journal consists of thirty-five folios, eight half-folios being left blank, and includes three charts. His handwriting is small, neat and quite mature for a young man in his early twenties. Like many of his contemporaries, he tends to use short dashes rather than full stops and frequently does not bother with either. Although Burney's spelling is reasonably good, considering his lack of formal education, his use of capital letters is erratic.

[1] T. C. Dale, The Society of Genealogists, *The Times Literary Supplement*, 10 December 1931.
[2] Charles Lamb to William Wordsworth, 20 March 1822, in Ainger, *Letters of Lamb*, Vol. II, p. 41.
[3] *The Times*, 20 November 1821.
[4] *Log*, 18 November 1772–23 January 1774. *Journal*, 19 November 1772–20 May 1774. PRO Adm. 51/4523.
[5] MS 3244, National Library of Australia.

Towards the end, the journal deteriorates into hastily written, disconnected notes and it seems possible that he originally intended to rewrite it on his return to England.

Burney begins his private journal with a description of the *Resolution's* uneventful passage to the Cape of Good Hope, where he was transferred to the *Adventure* as second lieutenant. The major phases of the *Adventure's* subsequent voyage, as described by Burney, are the passage south across the Antarctic Circle; the separation of the ships and the *Adventure's* solo voyage to Tasmania, where Burney led the first British landing ashore; the stay at Queen Charlotte Sound in New Zealand waiting for the *Resolution*; the cruise to the Society Islands and Tonga; the *Adventure's* prolonged battle to enter Cook Strait on the return to New Zealand, resulting in her permanent separation from the *Resolution*; and the final period in Queen Charlotte Sound, culminating in the tragedy of the Grass Cove massacre, before the *Adventure's* departure for England.

'My chief aim is your amusement,' Burney told his readers soon after the start of the voyage.[1] He wrote consciously for his family and friends, explaining naval terms they might not understand and, with the delicate feelings of his sisters in mind, avoiding detailed descriptions of distasteful customs and unpleasant incidents. He did not, for example, discuss in detail the sexual morals of the Society Islanders, a favourite topic for most journal-writers. Nor did he describe the massacre of ten of the *Adventure's* crew at Grass Cove. As leader of the expedition which found the men's remains, Burney's report on the massacre was probably his greatest contribution to the written material on Cook's second voyage. For this reason, it is included as an appendix.

Burney's private journal reflects the interests of a young sailor visiting the Pacific for the first time. Life at sea was no novelty to Burney and seemed scarcely worthy of comment. The highlight of the voyage, so far as he was concerned, was the encounter with the native inhabitants of the area—the Maoris, Society Islanders and Tongans. Voyagers from Tasman to Cook had already observed and described in detail the appearance, dress and customs of the Pacific Islanders and Burney adds little that is new, his observations reflecting largely what he had read in earlier journals and heard from fellow officers. On the Society Islands,

[1] See p. 25

an original source of information was Omai, the young native whom Furneaux took back to England in the *Adventure*. Although Burney learnt some of Omai's language on the homeward voyage, his ability to understand Omai at this early stage of their acquaintance must be suspect. Apart from the language problem, Burney himself thought that Omai was given to romancing and doubted the truth of some of his stories. An original contribution by Burney, reflecting his family background, is the setting out of Tongan and New Zealand tunes in musical notation.

If Burney reveals little original insight into places and peoples, neither does he reveal a great deal of himself as a person. Beaglehole claims that the journal 'gives us an unbuttoned Burney';[1] yet Burney does not really unbutton himself, even in this private work. His private journal is, indeed, more formal and aloof than the official logs and journals of some of the other young men on the voyage, lacking the liveliness of Second Lieutenant Charles Clerke's observations and the colourful language of Third Lieutenant Richard Pickersgill.[2] Only now and again does Burney allow a personal note to slip into his narrative. His obvious admiration for the Society Islanders shows that, even as a young man, he had sufficient breadth of vision to accept codes of behaviour different from the European model. His sympathy for the local natives, his own common sense and his impatience with the reckless behaviour of some of the other young men on the voyage are apparent from his suggestion that the Europeans were all too often to blame for the unpleasant—and sometimes fatal—confrontations between the two groups. At the same time, Burney makes a sustained effort to be impartial. While he is favourably impressed with the Society Islanders, he makes a point of recording what he considers to be their adverse features. Unlike many men of his time, he does not idolise the 'noble savage' at the expense of his critical powers.

In his continual concern for objectivity, Burney reveals himself as an honest young man with a down-to-earth, non-romantic view of the world and his fellow human beings. But while he was at sea he could not forget that he was first and foremost a naval officer;

[1] Beaglehole, *Cook Journals*, II, pp. cxxxviii–ix. Burney's private journal is referred to by Beaglehole as the 'Ferguson MS'.
[2] C. Clerke, *Log*, PRO Adm. 55/103; R. Pickersgill, *Log*, PRO Adm. 51/4553. Extracts from Clerke's and Pickersgill's writings are printed in Beaglehole, *Cook Journals*, II, pp. 753–75.

he could not 'unbutton' himself sufficiently even to demonstrate the liveliness and keen sense of humour that his sister, Fanny, wrote about in her diary. Burney's private journal, like his other writings, also reveals that he lacked the creative gifts with which other members of the Burney family were endowed. In compensation, he demonstrates a keen spirit of enquiry and an ability to express himself clearly and concisely. Forty years later, these features of Burney's work helped to make him one of the leading geographers of his day. The value of the journal-letter lies not so much in the material it presents as in the fact that it represents the early work of a member of a prominent English family who himself became famous in his later years.

BEVERLEY HOOPER
*Department of History*
*Australian National University*

# JAMES BURNEY'S
# PRIVATE JOURNAL

The Dispute between Mr Banks & the Captain, the Alteration of the Ship & all that happend before, you have been informd of by News papers & otherwise.[1] I shall therefore take my Departure from Sheerness whence we saild June 22$^d$ 1772 for Plymouth in order to join our Consort the Adventure.

June 25$^{th}$ Anchord this afternoon in the Downs, where we staid just long enough to provide ourselves with a little grogg & then Weighd Anchor—In our passage to Plymouth we tried M$^r$ Irwins Machine for making Salt Water fresh & found we could get near 15 Quarts per Hour[2]—

[1] Joseph Banks, the wealthy young botanist who had sailed on Cook's first voyage, intended accompanying Cook in the *Resolution*. His proposed retinue totalled fifteen, including the naturalist Dr Solander, the artist Zoffany, draughtsmen, secretaries, horn-players and servants. Banks insisted that the *Resolution* be altered to provide suitable accommodation for himself and his entourage. When the alterations, including an additional upper deck, had been completed, the ship was so top-heavy that Cook considered it unsafe and had it restored to its original condition. As a result, Banks refused to sail on the voyage and instead took his party to Iceland.—J. C. Beaglehole (ed.), *The Endeavour Journal of Joseph Banks, 1768–1771* (2 vols, Sydney, 1962), Vol. I, pp. 71–83; J. C. Beaglehole (ed.), *The Journals of Captain James Cook on his Voyages of Discovery, II, The Voyage of the Resolution and Adventure 1772–1775* (Cambridge, 1961), pp. xxvi–xxxii, 4–8.

[2] Dr Charles Irving's apparatus produced fresh water by condensing the steam from boiling salt water. When Cook tried Irving's 'machine', he found that the *Resolution's* coppers were 'not well addapted' for the purpose of distilling water. Despite its shortcomings, Cook was still using it three years later. On 21 June 1775 he stated it was 'upon the whole . . . a usefull invention' but advised 'no man to trust wholy to it'. While enough water could be obtained to support life, provided a ship had plenty of fuel and good coppers, 'you cannot, with all your efforts, obtain sufficient to support health, in hot

July 2ᵈ in the afternoon we met Lord Sandwich & Mr Palisser the Comptroller of the Navy, in the Augusta Yacht who came on board & Expressd much satisfaction at the Account he received of our Ship—next Morning we Anchord in Plymouth Sound where we found the Adventure—

Friday 10ᵗʰ this day our Ships Company receivd 7 months Pay to enable them to equip themselves for a long voyage & get drunk drinking success to it—

July 14ᵗʰ having compleated our Water, provisions, Stores etc. being provided with every thing necessary, we Weighd Anchor & Set Sail from Plymouth Sound in Company with the Adventure. At Noon we took our departure from the Ramhead of Plymouth which was the last English Land we saw—

And now I have got clear of England I will give you some Account of our Ships, Their force &c which by the bye oughts to have been done sooner—but it is not yet too late—we were 2 Ships, ours calld the Resolution carried 12 guns besides Swivels & 119 men including Captⁿ Cook[1] (whom hence-forward I shall call the Commodore) Dr Foster & Son, Botanists—Mr Hodge,[2] painter & Mr Wales, Astronomer—Our Consort the Adventure carried 10 Guns & 83 Men, commanded by Captⁿ Tobias Furneaux. There is an Astronomer likewise on board of her. There are in each Ship 2 Time Keepers, one made by Kendal & three by Arnold,[3] besides Astronomical Instruments of all kinds—by this account you may see we are not calculated to inspire Terror or to act offensively, nor shall we, I hope, have any occasion—what makes me take notice of this, is, its being one of

---

climates especially . . .'.—Beaglehole, *Cook Journals*, II, pp. 10, 10 n. 1, 672; The apparatus is described in C. J. Phipps, *A Voyage Towards the North Pole* (London, 1774), pp. 205–21 and Plate 14.

[1] Cook states 118. Beaglehole, *Cook Journals*, II, p. 12.
[2] William Hodges.
[3] In 1714 the Board of Longitude had offered a reward of £20,000 for an accurate method of determining longitude at sea. This was won by John Harrison who produced four chronometers between 1735 and 1761. A duplicate of his fourth model, made by London watchmaker Larcum Kendall, was carried on board the *Resolution*. 'Mr Kendall's watch', praised by Cook as 'our faithfull guide', proved highly successful and marked a turning-point in ocean navigation. The other three chronometers, made by John Arnold, broke down during the voyage.—Beaglehole, *Cook Journals*, II, pp. xxxix–xl, 692.

the Objections the Spaniards made to the Voyage[1]—One thing I must desire you to remember which is, as I intend to put down every thing that happens either at the very time, or within a day or two after, I shall write the same as if Speaking of the time present—now & then I may forget myself—you must make allowances.

Thursday July 23$^d$ in the Afternoon off Cape Finistere we met 9 Spanish Sail of the Line, one of them was an Admirals Ship with a Flag at his Mizen topmast Head. This brave fellow in a 74 gun Ship attended by 2 others, had the precaution first to pass us under English Colours near enough to see he might affront us with impunity, then boldly put about, hoisted Spanish Colours & fired 2 guns at our Consort to make us bring too and give an account of ourselves—nothing worth notice this Side of Madeira where we arrivd on the 28$^{th}$ at Night. We had the Satisfaction to find in this passage that the ship, though by many pronouncd incapable of going the Voyage, had the Advantage of the Adventure in several very material Articles—Sailing faster, having more room & being more able to carry Sail—Here we took in wines & filld our Empty Water Casks—The Island of Madeira belongs to the Portugueze, & lies in—Salmon's Geography or any other will tell you as well as I can, & I have not the least inclination to attempt a description of a place that so many have described before me. I am a poor hand at it & comparisons might not turn out to my credit. There are many things which it is necessary for a person to understand at least something of, that would wish to give an account of every place he sees, that I am utterly unacquainted with but poorly qualified as I am for a task of this nature, I am determined to wade through it, & in this resolution allow me to claim some little merit as my chief aim is your amusement—I am perswaded what I now write will never fall under the inspection of any who would wish to find fault, but will be read by those only who are predetermind to be pleasd. So much for my ignorance—the Voyage is young and good Company may mind me.

[1] Relations between England and Spain were strained, although the two countries had been officially at peace since the end of the Seven Years War in 1763. In January 1771 a quarrel over the Falkland Islands had almost erupted into war. Later the same year, the two ships for Cook's second voyage were commissioned as the *Drake* and the *Raleigh* but the Secretary of State requested the First Lord of the Admiralty to change the names because they would 'give great offence to the Spaniards'.—Lord Rochford to Lord Sandwich, 20 December 1771. Printed in Beaglehole, *Cook Journals*, II, p. 908.

August 1st At Night Weighd Anchor & left Madeira—4.<sup>th</sup> & 5<sup>th</sup> passed the Canary Islands.

Thursday 13<sup>th</sup> in the Afternoon we anchord at St Iago one of the Cape de Verd Islands in possession of the Portugueze here we recruited our Water, & Supplied our Selves with Live Stock, Vegetables & plenty of Fruit which we purchasd for Old Cloaths —the Inhabitants are, except the Portugueze, mostly black— they live on Indian Corn & Fruit whilst their Habitations are surrounded with fat Hogs, Goats, Fowls & all kinds of good things.

August 15<sup>th</sup> We Saild from S<sup>t</sup> Iago—N.B. Water here bad.

Thursday 20<sup>th</sup> One of our Capenters Mates, Henry Smock, being at work on the Outside of the Ship, the Weather being very fine, fell overboard without being perceivd & was unfortunately drownd before any of us knew any thing of the Matter.

27<sup>th</sup> Spoke the Adventure who informed us of the death of one of their Midshipmen—that they had been sickly Since they left St Iago but were now all well—

Monday September 7<sup>th</sup> Saw a Sail to the S.W<sup>t</sup> but did not come near enough to Speak her, or see what she was. This Afternoon a remarkable cause was tried by the Commodore—2 of the Men by way of Fun made an house of Office of a pair of Breeches belonging to our Armourer which he finding out complaind of the Fact being fully provd the Aggressors were obligd between them to buy the Breeches, each paying an equal Share. They then tossd up which should keep them & the Winner was orderd on the Spot to try how his new purchase fitted; which, after many wry faces, he did, to the no small diversion of the Spectators, many Jokes, or what were meant as Such being made on the Occasion— This Night we crossd the Equinox, & the next day performd the usual ceremony of ducking those who had never been this way before—this day we fell in with the S.E<sup>t</sup> Trades—

Tuesday 15<sup>th</sup> being fine Weather Sent our Boat on board the Adventure—found they had lost another of their Midshipmen by a Fever.

Monday 28.ᵗʰ Saw a Sail to the Westward, standing the Same way we did, under Portugueze Colours—

October 29.ᵗʰ this Afternoon Saw the Land & next Morning Anchord in Table Bay at the Cape of Good Hope. here we compleated our Water, & provisions. I shall enter into no description of this place now, I may probably be better qualified to say something about it when we come back—

Wednesd. November 18.ᵗʰ on this good day I left the Resolution being appointed 2.ᵈ Lieutenant of the Adventure in the room of M.ʳ Shanks who quitted on account of his health[1]—On Sunday 22.ᵈ we Weighd Anchor & Saild out of the Bay. Next morning we lost Sight of the Land—& now I look on the Voyage as begun & not before[2]—

Monday 23.ᵈ This day both Ships Company's were servd Magellan Jackets & Trowsers, being a present from the Government—we now made the best of our way to the Southward to look for Cape Circumcision, which Mons.ʳ Bouvet has laid down in 54°S° Lat.ᵈᵉ & 9° or 10° E.ᵗ Longitude from London[3]—the Remainder of this month & great part of the next had continual hard gales of Wind & very boisterous weather—December 7th Saw some Sea Weed & a great many Sea Birds, being in 49° S° Lat.ᵈᵉ

December 10.ᵗʰ this morning we fell in with an Island of Ice which at first we mistook for Land—in the afternoon we saw another & 2 penguins, Birds which are said never to be far from Land. we

---

[1] This was not entirely accurate. Burney replaced Arthur Kempe, the *Adventure's* second lieutenant, who was promoted to first lieutenant when Joseph Shank left the ship to return to England. Shank, who suffered from gout, had been confined to his cabin for several weeks on the voyage to the Cape.—Cook to Stephens, 18 November 1772. *Historical Records of New South Wales*, I, i, pp. 368–72; Beaglehole, *Cook Journals*, II, pp. 44, n. 5, 47–8.

[2] Burney meant that Cook could now pursue his major objective: to prove or disprove the existence of a southern continent.

[3] On 1 January 1739, Lozier Bouvet, a French East India Company captain, had sighted a rocky, snow-bound cape in the South Atlantic, slightly west of the Cape of Good Hope. He named his discovery Cape Circumcision. Although Bouvet caught only a glimpse of land through the fog, he thought it might be part of a great southern continent.—James Burney, *A Chronological History of the Discoveries in the South Sea or Pacific Ocean* (5 vols, London, 1803–17), Vol. 5, pp. 32–4; Beaglehole, *Cook Journals*, II, pp. lii–liii.

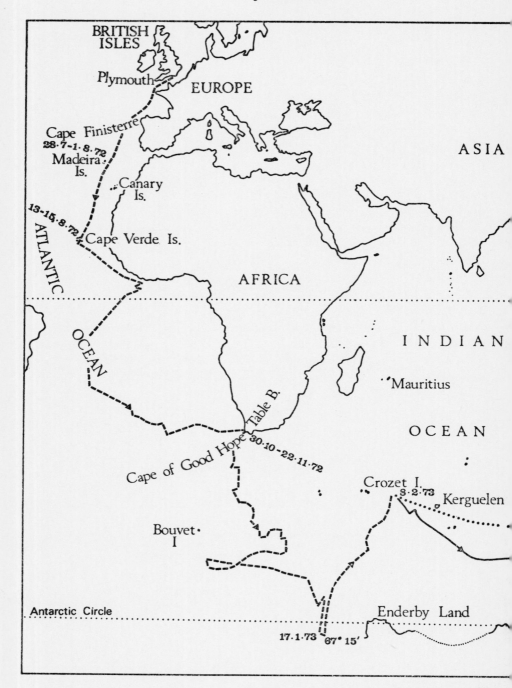

Fig. 1. The track of t▌

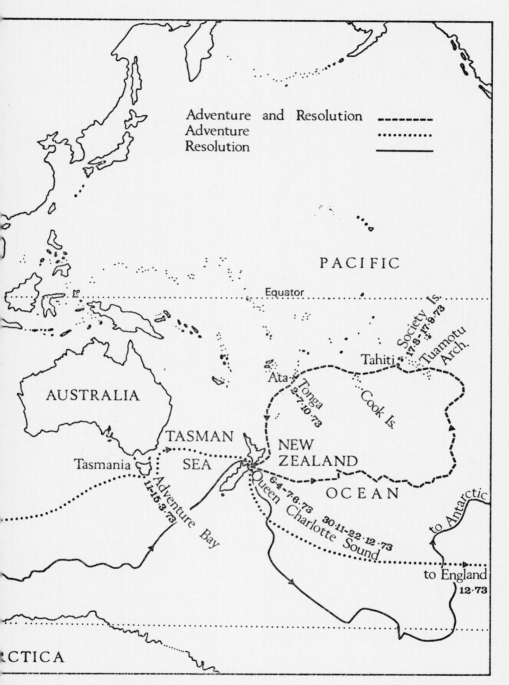

and *Adventure*, 1772–3.

tried Soundings but got no ground. After this we passd great quantities of Ice every day—the Weather very cold, though near Midsummer at this part of the World—The quick silver in the Thermometer keeping constantly between 27½ & 32—

The Ice we meet with at Sea is distinguished by 2 different Names, Islands & Fields, though in fact they are all Islands. The Fields of Ice are low & level—& are many Leagues in length— we have saild close by one above 6 Leagues without being able to get a passage through, or Seeing the End of it. The Islands are very high rugged pieces, Seldom more than half a mile in Length & are about 150 feet high from the Surface of the Water. There are some of the largest Islands at least as high as S.t Pauls—I only Saw 2 of this enormous height, one of them I am certain was much higher.* These Islands seem to change Colour as the Weather changes—When the Sun Shines & the Sky is clear they are of a fine light blue & transparent, in bad dirty weather they resemble Land coverd with Snow the lower part appearing black. If a Ship should run against a large piece of Ice I make no doubt but she would receive as much damage as from a Rock—

Dec.ber 13.th We were now in the Latitude of Cape Circumcision, but near 100 Leagues E.t of it, the Winds blowing almost constantly from the Westward. for 3 days after this we fell in with so much Ice that we were obliged to run to the Eastward for fear of being blockd up. We Saw great numbers of Whales & Sea Birds every day but no Sign of any Land—the 24th the Wind came round to the N.E. & we again Steerd to the S.W.tward—the Fields of Ice now began to seperate & we frequently found passages through them.

1773 January 2.d we were now nearly in the Long.de of Cape Circumcision, but to the Southward; being in 59 degrees South Latitude—no Signs of Land—Bouvet himself was not Sure he saw Land, he only says he saw something that had the appearance of it, but could not get near enough to be certain for the Ice. Bouvet was to the Westward when he first Saw it & then ran to the Northward of it we have been due East & due South from it so that our Tracks put together would almost circumscribe the place very likely if we come back round Cape Horn we may take

* *Ice floating in the Sea is said to be only 1/4th. above the Surface.*

another Cruize for Cape Circumcision which will determine whether it be real or imaginary—the Wind now coming to the N.W. a fresh Gale and likely to continue we on the 4th Steerd to the S.E.[1]—

January 9th being very fine Weather we brought too by an Island of Ice & hoisted our Boats out to pick up the loose pieces to water the Ship—we got 6 Boat Loads which when melted in the Coppers gave us 7 Tons of Excellent fresh water—

Jan[ry] 12th This day we again hoisted our boats out & got Ice enough to fill all our Empty Casks—have more water than when we left the Cape of Good Hope. We were now in 64 degrees South Latitude—Weather better & warmer than before—the Season being more advancd. We have had daylight the whole 24 Hours round, for some time past.

Sunday 17th This Forenoon we crossd the Antartic Circle being in 40°. . 22′ E[t] Longitude from Greenwich[2]—in the afternoon we fell in with a great deal of Ice, & at 7 were in the midst of a Loose Field. our Horizon from the S.E. round to W.S.W. was entirely coverd with Ice. We Tackd not being able to get farther without running very great risks—the Season was now too far advancd

---

[1] Furneaux had begun to 'doubt if there was any such place'. If there was, it 'must be some inconsiderable spot not habitable by reason of the intense cold'. Cook had more positively concluded that there was no land in the area and that 'what M. Bouvet took for Land and named Cape Circumcision was nothing but Mountains of Ice surrounded by field Ice'. He was 'only sorry that in searching after those imaginary Lands ... [he had] spent so much time, which will become the more valuable as the season advanceth'. Furneaux was nearer the truth: Cape Circumcision did exist, not as part of a great continent but as the north-west extremity of a tiny island (now called Bouvet Island), five miles by four miles. There was no other land within a radius of one thousand miles. Bouvet had made a longitudinal error of approximately eight degrees when he gave the Cape's position as 54°10–15′S, 11°20′E. Its correct location was 54°26′S, 3°24′E.—T. Furneaux, *Account of the Adventure's Voyage* (B.M. Add. MS 27890). Extracts from this journal are printed as *Furneaux's Narrative* in Beaglehole, *Cook Journals*, II, pp. 729–45; Beaglehole, *Cook Journals*, II, pp. lii–liii, 71–2, 730.

[2] The *Resolution* and *Adventure* were the first ships to cross the Antarctic Circle. Cook wrote in his journal: 'At about a ¼ past 11 o'Clock we cross'd the Antarctic Circle for at Noon we were by observation four Miles and a half South of it and are undoubtedly the first and only Ship that ever cross'd that line'. He did not mention the *Adventure*.—Beaglehole, *Cook Journals*, II, p. 80.

for us to attempt getting nearer the Pole. When we put about we were in 67°.. 11′ South Latitude.[1]

There was a report at the Cape of 2 French Ships having discoverd Land due South from the Island Mauritius in the Latitude of 49 or 50 degrees. as this was not a great deal out of our Rout to New Holland we Steerd to the N.E. in hopes of finding it—by the End of this Month we almost got clear of the Ice.

Jan^ry 30^th In Lat^de 51..20S° & Longitude 56° East from the Meridian of Greenwich. This afternoon had a Stiff Gale of Wind from the Northward. The Water remarkably Smooth the next day passd 2 Islands of Ice—

February 1^st were this morning due South from the Island of Mauritius, our Latitude being 49° S°. Wind N.N.W. water still smooth though it blew very fresh. This afternoon we Saw a great deal of Sea Weed & some Divers (Birds which are never seen far from Land)—I imagine by the Smoothness of the Water these 2 day past & what we saw this afternoon that there is Land to the Westward—We made the signal to Speak the Commodore & informd him of what we saw—we cruised hereabouts till the 6th without seeing any Land though we daily Saw numbers of Birds & pieces of Sea Weed—we frequently tried Soundings but got no ground—the Wind all this time blew so fresh from the N.W. that we could not get to the Westward but on the contrary lost ground —on the 6th the wind increasing without the least prospect of a Change we bore away for New Holland which was yet near 4000 miles from us[2]—

---

[1] For the reasons Burney states, Cook had decided not to push farther south: 'I did not think it was consistant with the safty of the Sloops or any ways prudent for me to persevere in going farther to the South as the summer was already half spent and it would have taken up some time to have got round this Ice, even supposing this to have been practicable, which however is doubtfull.' Cook correctly suspected that he was not far from land. The Prince Olav Coast of the Antarctic Continent was about seventy-five miles away but, according to Beaglehole, 'it is most improbable that Cook could have reached it'. The ships were, in fact, south of part of the Antarctic Continent. Had they sailed for a short distance to the east, instead of returning immediately north, they would have sighted the Tula Mountains of Enderby Land.—Beaglehole, *Cook Journals*, II, pp. 81, 81 n. 2.

[2] In February 1772, a Frenchman, Yves Joseph de Kerguelen-Trémarec, had sighted land on a voyage south from Mauritius. The land, a small island, was located approximately seven degrees to the east of the position given by Kerguelen (63°30′E). In December 1776, on his third voyage, Cook found the

I believe there are some Islands hereabouts, but no Land of any great Extent—for Tasmans track, ours, & the track in which our Outward bound China Ships commonly Sail in war time, circumscribe the place & if here had been any large tract of Land Some of us must have seen it.[1]

Monday February 8th this morning at 9, the Resolution being a head of us about a mile it came on so foggy that we lost Sight of each other—soon after the wind shifting we knew not which way to act to prevent parting Company—at 10 we heard a gun which they had fired, this we answerd, but were now more puzzled than ever as Some asserted the Sound came from the S.W. & others from the Eastward—in short though we fired guns every half hour till the Weather cleard up, we could neither see nor hear any thing of her—at 3 in the Afternoon we thought we saw her to the S.S.E. on which we made all the Sail we could that way, but at 5 it cleard up a little & we Saw nothing. after this we endeavourd to get back to the Spot where we parted, but the wind blew so fresh from the N.W. that at the end of 3 days we found ourselves 17 Leagues to Leeward, we therefore bore away again for New Holland. When we parted, were in 50 degrees S°. Latitude & 63 degrees East Long$^{de}$ reckoning from Greenwich.

As Captain Cook intended running to the Southward as far as 55° S°. Captain Furneaux thought it most adviseable to Slant to the Southward to 52° 30 S°. & then haul again to the Nward by degrees till we should be in the Latitude of Van Diemen's Land. This was keeping nearly in the middle between Capt$^n$. Cook and Tasman, & by Sailing in 2 different routs we should be less liable to miss anything in our way.[2]

---

island and called it the Island of Desolation because of its lack of vegetation. It was later renamed Kerguelen Land (Island).—M. de Kerguelen, *Relation de Deux Voyages dans les Mers Australes & des Indies, faits en 1771, 1772, 1773 & 1774* (Paris, 1782), pp. 21–5; Beaglehole, *Cook Journals*, II, pp. liii–liv; III, p. 43.

[1] Burney was correct. The ships were approximately midway between two islands (Crozet Island and Kerguelen Island) situated about one thousand miles apart in the southern Indian Ocean.

[2] After searching unsuccessfully for the *Adventure* for two days, Cook set his course for New Zealand where he wanted to find a suitable southern port before joining the *Adventure* at Queen Charlotte Sound, the appointed rendezvous. Cook also intended to visit Van Diemen's Land en route but north-west winds forced him to change his mind and he sailed direct to New Zealand, arriving at Dusky Sound on 26 March 1773.—Beaglehole, *Cook Journals*, II, pp. 92–109.

Feb^ry 14^th. Saw 2 Seals & a progidious Number of Birds.

21^st. Saw an Is^d of Ice this Morning—

Monday March 1^st at 7 in the Morning thought we saw Land to the Northward, but by the time we had run 15 miles that way it disappeard—

Tuesday March 9^th Saw. the Land at 9 this Forenoon bearing N.N.E., this is Van Demen's Land first discovered by Abel Tasman in 1642—it lays South of New Holland if not joining— the Wind being at N.W. we hauld close up for the Land—Got our Anchors and Cables ready—at Noon the Extremes of the Land bore from N.E. W. to E.N.E.—from the Northernmost Land in Sight it trenches away about S.E. & S.S.E. to a bluff Point that we calld the S.W. Cape. Whence the Land runs nearly East— Several small Islands along shore which Tasman calls the Pedra blancs—Lat^de Observd 43..45S^o & Long^de 146..20 E^t1—

The 2 next days I shall write the Ships Log on one Side & my own remarks on the other—the Log can be no kind of Entertainment to you, but may be of use to me in case my Journal is not returned me; and you may easily Skip it—

---

[1] These were the first of Furneaux's errors in identifying the Tasmanian coastline, whereby he continually located his position too far east in relation to the chart drawn by Abel Janszoon Tasman, who had discovered the island in 1642. The mistakes began when Furneaux thought the cape he called South-West Cape was the one Tasman had called South Cape. (To confuse matters, Burney labelled it S.W. Cape, not South Cape, on his drawing of Tasman's chart.) In fact, Tasman's South Cape was farther east, corresponding to what Furneaux called South-East Cape. Furneaux consequently thought that Tasman's Maatsuyker Islands were the Pedra Brancka (Blanca) Islands, also located farther east. When Cook visited Tasmania on his third voyage in January 1777, he accepted Furneaux's nomenclature, some of which has been retained to the present day.—See T. Furneaux, *Journal*, PRO Adm. 55/1, entries for 10–19 March 1773; Cook's comments on Furneaux's observations in Beaglehole, *Cook Journals*, II, pp. 161–5; and Andrew Sharp, *The Voyages of Abel Janszoon Tasman* (Oxford, 1968), p. 109. The discrepancies between Furneaux's and Tasman's nomenclatures are discussed by Beaglehole, *Cook Journals*, II, pp. 149–53, and III, pp. 49–50, 56–7.

| Hours | Miles | Furl$^{gs}$ | Courses | Winds | Wednesd. March 10$^{th}$ 1773 |
|---|---|---|---|---|---|
| 1 | 2 | 6 | NNE | NNW | Little wind and Hazy |
| 2 | 2 | 4 | NEbE | NW | hoisted out the smallCutter & |
| 3 | 3 | 3 | EBN | | sent her in Shore—at ½ p$^t$ 2 |
| 4 | 3 | 4 | | | fired a gun for her to return |
| | | | | | Fresh Breezes & fair— |
| 5 | 2 | ,, | | | Sounded 47 fathom. Coral & |
| | | | | | broken shells— |
| 6 | 1 | 6 | | WSW | Sounded ground at 47 fm. as |
| 7 | 1 | 4 | | | before Var$^{tn}$ pr Az$^{th}$ 7..02 E$^t$ |
| 8 | 2 | ,, | SE | ENE | abrest the Mewstone it bear- |
| | | | | | ing S$^o$ 2 miles |
| 9 | 2 | 4 | East | NNE | S.W$^t$ Cape W.B.N. ¼N. |
| 10 | 2 | ,, | | | Soundings all the first Watch |
| 11 | 1 | 6 | | | between 50 & 60 fms fine |
| | | | | | brown Sand & Shells— |
| 12 | 2 | 4 | | WBS | |
| 1 | 1 | 4 | | | |
| 2 | 1 | 4 | EBN | NbW | fair Weather |
| 3 | 1 | ,, | NEBN | NW | |
| 4 | ,, | ,, | — | Calm | |
| 5 | 2 | ,, | SEBE | NEBE | Light breezes and fair—Tackd |
| 6 | 3 | ,, | NNW | NE | Mewstone W½S 4 or 5 Leagues |
| | | | | | —E.ermost Land in Sight |
| 7 | 3 | ,, | North | Variable | |
| | | | | | N.E. this we call the S.E. Cape |
| | | | | | —lays E.N.E. from the |
| | | | | | MewstoneRock— |
| 8 | 1 | 4 | NNE | | Var$^{tn}$ pr Amp$^d$ 7..13 E$^t$ pr Az$^{th}$. |
| | | | | | 7..01 E$^t$ |
| 9 | 1 | ,, | — | | Hoisted the large Cutter out & |
| 10 | 1 | 2 | | | sent her in Shore |
| 11 | 1 | 4 | | | at 11 Strong Gales & Squally— |

up NNW of North

12

up S ½ off SSE—

Fired several Guns as Sig-
nals for the Boat to return
wore Ship & *Batton* Close
Reefd the Fore and main S$^l$
& Handed the Mizen Top-
sail.

At Noon the S.E$^t$ Cape bore E.N.E. about 7 miles—No Observances Lat$^{de}$ pr Au$^t$ 43..38S$^o$. Diff$^{ce}$ of Long$^{de}$ this 24 hours O$^o$. 56° E I allow more distance than the Log gives for a Swell from the Westward—

| Hours | Miles | Furl$^{gs}$ | Courses | Winds | |
|---|---|---|---|---|---|
| 1 | — | — | — | West | Fresh Gales and Hazy—at $\frac{1}{2}$ |
| 2 | 5 | 2 | EBN | WSW | past 12 the Boat returnd— |
| 3 | 5 | 2 | | | hoisted her in & Bore away. |
| 4 | 5 | 5 | NEbE$\frac{1}{2}$E | | Out 3$^d$ Reef Main tops$^l$. |
| 5 | 6 | 4 | NE | | abrest the N.E. point of Storm Bay |
| 6 | 6 | 4 | NbE | | |
| 7 | 2 | 5 | North | | Anchord in the Skirts of a fine Bay with the Small Bower in |
| | 2 | 3 | NW | | 24 fm—Clay and Mudd— |

At 2 this afternoon being little wind, hoisted out the small Cutter & sent her in shore with the Master—$\frac{1}{2}$ an hour after a fresh breeze Springing up made a Signal for her to return had Soundings all the first part of the Night between 50 & 60 fms at 5 in the Morning we Stood in Shore—at $\frac{1}{2}$ past 6 we passed a fine deep Bay with several Islands in it (2 Peaks to the E$^t$w$^d$ of it) at 9 being little wind the large Cutter was hoisted out & I was sent in her to see if I could find any fresh Water—we rowd in shore a little to the Eastward of the Bay just mentiond—We Observd the Land seemd to part which made me conjecture there was a fresh water river, but it was too far from the Ship for me to think of going thither by 11 we got into a Small Bay where we saw a Sandy beach but could not land for the Surf—however we soon found a good Landing place on some Rocks. The first thing we saw when we climbed up was a heap of wood ashes, the remains of a fire which had been kindled there & a great number of Pearl Scollop Shells. We saw no inhabitants, there was a very good path leading into the woods which would probably have led us to some of their Huts, but we could not stay to walk up, the Wind coming too fresh obligd us to think of getting on board again. We brought off Several Boughs of Trees, some shells & some of the burnt wood. at the Entrance of this Bay on the East Side was a fine fall of water among the Rocks, but not safe for the Boat to come near it. by

Plate 1. Admiral Burney,
'Drawn from a Bust and Engraved by Rich^d H. Dyer' (detail).
Reproduced by courtesy of the
National Maritime Museum, Greenwich.

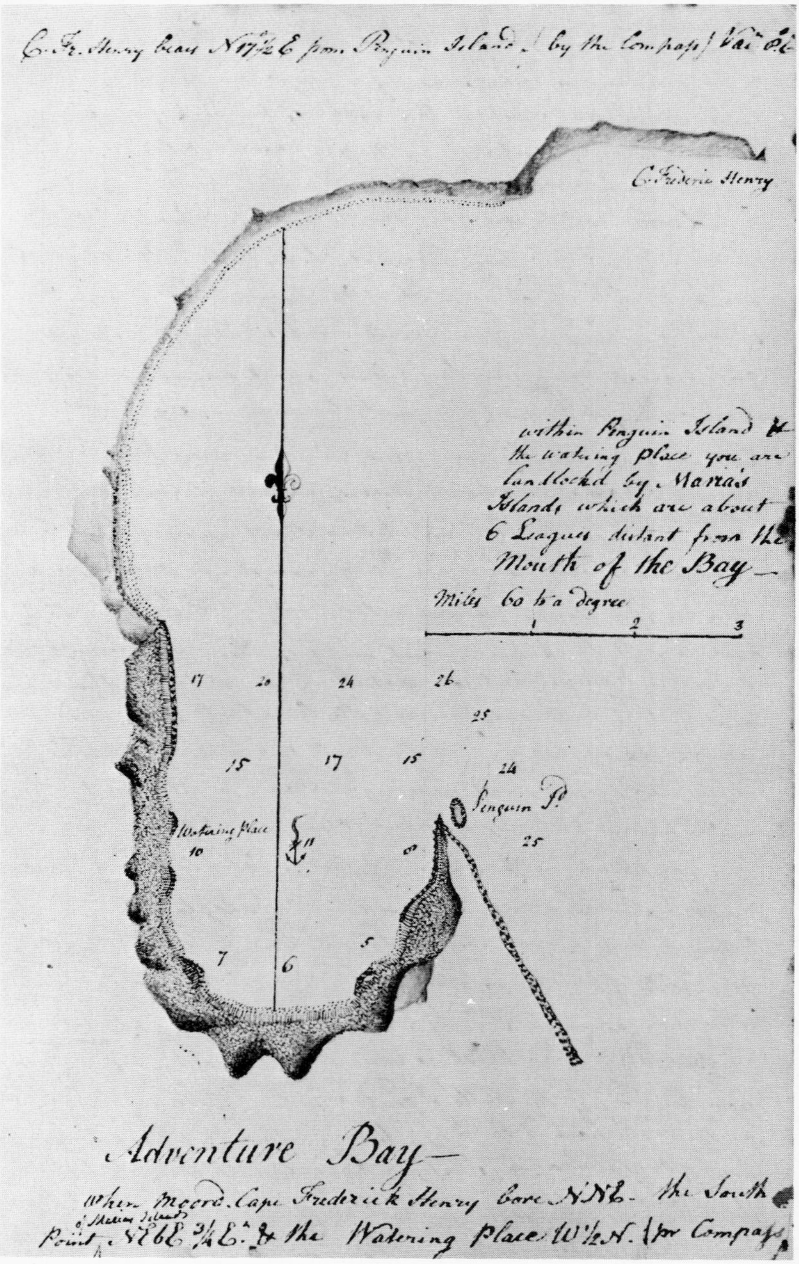

Plate 2. Burney's chart of Adventure Bay,
reproduced from his private journal.

3/4 of an hour past noon we got safe on board[1]—by this time it blew a Fresh Gale from the WSW which had obligd the Ship to close Reef the Topsails & furl the Mizen Topsail—at 1 we Bore away having hoisted the Boat in—the Shore seems very bold (Steep) affording plenty of good Bays and Harbours all along the Coast. The Land is every where coverd with trees making one continued Wood—at ½ past 1 were abrest the S.E.t Cape which makes the S.W. point of Storm Bay[2]—at 5 were abrest of Tasmans Head[3]—Several Rocks & small Islands close to it which we named the Fryars—at 7 we anchord in the Skirts of a fine Bay— the Wind abating we lay Safely here all Night—& next morning at daylight Sent the Master with 2 Boats to Sound and look for a Watering place—

Thursday March 11th As Soon as the Boats returned we weighd with a light breeze from the Westward & began to turn up the Bay where we anchord in the Afternoon & Moord the Ship— Many on board supose this to be Frederick Henry's Bay, but from Several Circumstances I am perswaded to the Contrary. Tasman lays down Frederick Henrys Bay in 43..10S.o Lat.de 9 Leagues distant in a direct line from the N.E.t point of Storm Bay & makes it 9 or 10 Leagues deep from the Entrance—this which we namd Adventure Bay is in 43..20 S.o only 3 Leagues from Tasmans Head & is not more then 3 miles deep from the Entrance to the Bottom of the Bay—Tasman in his Chart has laid down a small Nook or Inlet to the Southward of Frederic Henrys Bay which exactly corresponds with this[4]—

[1] Burney's excursion ashore, in charge of nine seamen, was the first British landing in Tasmania. Since the island's discovery by Tasman in 1642 it had been visited only once: by Marion du Fresne in March 1772, almost exactly a year before the *Adventure*. The site of the landing was on Tasmania's south coast, slightly to the west of South-East Cape. (See Burney's chart, p. 52.)
[2] South-East Cape was not the south-west point of Storm Bay, but of d'Entrecasteaux Channel which separates the Tasmanian mainland from Bruni Island.
[3] The *Adventure* was off the south-east point of Bruni Island, not the south-east point of Tasman Peninsula as Furneaux thought.
[4] Burney, like Furneaux, wrongly concluded that the bay in which the *Adventure* was anchored, named by Furneaux Adventure Bay, was on the eastern side of Tasman Peninsula. He consequently charted it immediately south of Tasman's Frederick Henry Bay (now Blackman's Bay). Adventure Bay was, in fact, on the eastern side of Bruni Island and corresponded to Tasman's Storm Bay.

Friday 12<sup>th</sup>. Early this morning we sent our Boats on shore to the South Side of the Bay for Wood & Water with a party of marines to guard them. found the Water very brackish (Salt) in the Afternoon we found another Watering place the Water Something better. at Night we hauld the Sean on shore and caught some fish. have seen no Inhabitants as yet—

Sunday 14<sup>th</sup>. found a Small River with a fine run of excellent fresh water on the West Side of the Bay—it lays WBS from a Small Island off the South point of the Bay. this Island we calld Penguin Island from our catching one of those birds there—

The whole time we staid here we did not get a Sight of any of the Inhabitants, though they were so near that we saw fires continually on the North Side the Bay where the Land is lower, more level & not so much overrun with Wood as the part we lay in. we found Several of their Huts & large old Hollow Trees in which they had lived. there were paths which led along the woods, but almost overgrown with Bushes. the place did not seem to have been inhabited for some Months before, so that it was not our coming frightend them away. it is most likely the Natives never Stay long in one place but lead a Wandering Life, travelling along the Coast from Bay to Bay to catch fish, which by the great quantities of Shell we saw, must make the chief part of their food. their Huts are very low and ill contrived & seem only intended for temporary habitations. They had left nothing in them but 2 or 3 Baskets or Bags made of a very Strong Grass—Some flints and tinder which I believe they make of the bark of a Tree, & a great Number of Pearl Scollop, Mussel, Lobster, & Crayfish shells which they had roasted—

This Land is Situated in a fine, temperate & healthy Climate the Country is exceeding Pleasant, but almost impassible to penetrate into it on account of the Woods; nor is it very safe Walking. here are some small snakes, one of which we caught and a great many very large Ants about an inch and a half long— they bite most confoundedly, and are very troublesome—

The Trees are mostly Evergreens, Standing very thick & close. many of the Small ones bore berries of a Spicy flavour. the large Trees are in general quite Strait, & Shoot up very high before they branch out. They are large enough for masts for any Ship in the Navy. but are rather brittle and heavy. they have a soft thick bark which many of them had been strippd of by the Natives, but for what use I cannot tell—there is a great deal of What our Surgeon calls Gum lock in the Wood, which Tasman takes notice of[1]—at the back of some of the Sandy beaches are small Lagoons or Lakes with good Store of Trout, Carp & other fish. here is likewise plenty of Wild fowl & Game, but so Shy that I imagine the Natives have some method of Catching them. We Shot some Wild Ducks, Crows, Parraquets, a White Eagle, one of the finest looking fellows I ever saw, & some small birds— we saw the tracks of Wild Beasts along the Sand—One of our Gentlemen Shot a Possown, about the Size of a Cat which was the only Animal we saw here—this beast is very common in America—

from the Tops of the Hills I could See Water beyond the Lowland at the North part of the Bay, but whether this has communication with the Sea, or is only a Lagoon we could not determine if the former it must doubtless be the Bay of Frederick Henry we could see the Land again beyond this water[2]—it seems to be a fine country to the Northward & by the many fires we saw there must be well inhabited—it is very remarkable that no European has ever seen an Inhabitant of Van Diemens Land—& it is now more than 130 years since it was first discoverd[3]—

[1] Tasman reported in his journal on 2 December 1642, the date of the first European landing in Tasmania, that the landing party had seen 'fine Gum which is dripping from trees, and has an Odour of Gommalacca'. The trees described by Tasman and Burney were eucalypts. Their bark, especially that of the Stringy-bark (Eucalyptus oblique) was used by the nomadic Aborigines to build simple huts, often no more than break-winds, and rafts.—Sharp, Voyages of Tasman, p. 110; H. Ling Roth, The Aborigines of Tasmania, second ed. (Halifax, 1899), pp. 108–11, 154–8.

[2] This was in accordance with Burney's opinion that the Adventure was anchored in a bay immediately south of Frederick Henry Bay. In fact, the stretch of water he saw was Isthmus Bay, part of d'Entrecasteaux Channel which separates Bruni Island from the mainland.

[3] Burney did not know that the Frenchman, Marion du Fresne, had visited Tasmania in March 1772 nor that his men had a hostile encounter with some Tasmanian Aborigines at Frederick Henry Bay. As a result of a misunderstanding, the Aborigines attacked the French with stones and spears. The French responded with musket fire, killing one Aboriginal and wounding several others. Burney himself saw some Tasmanian Aborigines almost four years later when he spent four days at Adventure Bay in January 1777 during Cook's third voyage. Unlike Marion, Burney found the Aborigines 'quite inoffensive'; they 'had no arms and seemed not in the least apprehensive or suspicious'.—Jas. A. Boosé (ed.), Crozet's Voyage to Tasmania, New Zealand, the Ladrone Islands, and the Philippines in the Years 1771–1772, trans. H. Ling Roth (London, 1891), pp. 18–20; J. Burney, Journal, PRO Adm. 51/4528, entry for 28 January 1777.

The Tide rises here not more than 3 or 4 feet perpendicular the Current or Set of it is scarcely perceptible. The Ship always tending to the wind, though ever so little of it. it was 9 days past the Full Moon when we came in, so that the Tides were then at the highest—

I made Penguin Rock by the South point of the Bay to be in 43°..20' S° Lat$^{de}$ & in 147°..45' E$^t$ Longitude from Greenwich by the Mean of Several good Observations of the Sun and Moon's Distance—

Variation 8°..00' E$^t$ Tasman found it 3° E$^t$ in the year 1642 When moord the North point of the Bay bore N.N.E. Easterly the South point N.E. b E.3/4 E.—& the Watering place W.$\frac{1}{2}$ N.— 11 fathom, Sandy Bottom—within Penguin Island & the Watering Place you are Landlockd by Maria's Islands which are about 6 Leagues distant from the Mouth of the Bay, laying nearly North & South of each other[1]. These Islands have a good promising appearance, & are inhabited; for we saw Smokes in the Vallies—

Monday March 15$^{th}$. this Morning, having compleated our Wood & Water, we left this Bay, Steering East to go to the Southward of Marias Islands—at Noon were E. B N.3/4 N. by the Compass from Penguin Island. distant about 5 miles Lat$^{de}$. Obs$^d$ 43°..19' South. After Sunset we steerd to the S.E$^t$ to get a good Offing (clear of the Land). Variation this evening 9..01 East—

Tuesday 16$^{th}$ at daylight this morning Bore away to the North-ward, Wind S.W., a fresh breeze with fair Weather. at Noon were abrest Maria's Islands, they bearing from N.W. $\frac{1}{4}$N. to S.W.B.W. Lat$^{de}$ Observd 43..08 S° Longitude made from Adventure Bay. 0°..5'6 E$^t$ from here I shall write down the Logg till we left the Land. what makes me so particular is this Land being so little known—no Ship having been here since it was first discoverd[2]—

---

[1] The land to the north-east was not 'Maria's Islands' but Tasman Peninsula. As Tasman had indicated on his chart, there was only one 'Maria's Island' (Maria Island), situated north-east of Tasman Peninsula.

[2] See note p. 39 n. 3. Both Tasman and Marion had left the Tasmanian coastline to sail to New Zealand without exploring its northern limits. Furneaux intended sailing north until he could determine whether or not Van Diemen's Land was part of the Australian continent.

| H. | Miles | Furl<sup>gs</sup>. | Courses | Winds | Wednesday March 17<sup>th</sup>. 1773— |
|---|---|---|---|---|---|
| 1 | 2 | 6 | NWbN | WbS | Mod<sup>t</sup> breezes and fair Weather—saw an Island to |
| 2 | 2 | 6 | | | the Northward of Maria's Islands, bearing N. b W.½ W. |
| 3 | 3 | 4 | | | this I take to be what Tasman calls Schoutens Island |
| 4 | 4 | " | | | |
| 5 | 4 | " | NNW | West | Variation 8..41 E<sup>t</sup> per Azimuth |
| 6 | 3 | 6 | NNE | NW | Northernmost of Maria's Islands N.W.b W. part of the Main Land within |
| 7 | 2 | 4 | NEbE | NbW | it N.W. b N. 12 or 14 Leagues |
| 8 | 2 | 6 | NEbN | NWbW | Shortend Sail |
| 9 | 3 | 3 | North | West | |
| 10 | 3 | " | | | |
| 11 | 3 | 2 | | | |
| 12 | 3 | " | | | Fresh breezes and Cloudy |
| 1 | 2 | 4 | — | WNW | |
| 2 | 2 | " | | | |
| 3 | 2 | 6 | NbW | WbN | |
| 4 | 3 | 4 | — | — | made Sail |
| 5 | 3 | 4 | NW½N | WSW | |
| 6 | 4 | " | — | — | the Southernmost of Schouten's Islands W. B S. ½ S. 4 or |
| 7 | 4 | 2 | | | 5 Leagues Northernmost N.W. b W. |
| 8 | 6 | " | NWbN | SSW | |
| 9 | 6 | 4 | | | |
| 10 | 6 | 6 | NNW | | At Noon the Extremes of the Land from the South |
| 11 | 6 | 6 | NWbN | | to N.W. b N. distance off Shore 3 or 4 miles— |
| 12 | 6 | 4 | — | South | |

Lat$^{de}$ Obs$^d$ 41..45S$^o$ Long$^{de}$ from Adventure Bay 0°..44' E. from Greenwich 148..29E$^t$—Schoutens Islands lay N. b W. & S. b E. of each other & they are 4 or 5 in number, very high Land & may be seen a great distance. when we were to the Southward of them they appeard like one Small Island for we had them all in a line. Tasman has laid down but one in his Chart—at ½ past 10 this forenoon were abrest a high headland to the Northward of the Islands this is part of the Main, & I believe is what Tasman calls Vanderlins Eyl[1]—from here the Land runs nearly N.N.W. by the Compass—falling in here and there in pretty deep Bays—Seemingly a bold Shore—Somewhere hereabouts Tasman left the Land. Thus far we have been much beholden to his chart which is an exceeding good one: especially if it be considerd how imperfect Navigation was at that time, & that he had a fresh of wind with thick dirty weather whilst he remaind on this Coast[2]. I look on Tasman to have been one of the ablist & most fortunate Voyagers of his time[3].

Tasman by dead Reckoning (Observations of the Sun & Moon for the Longitude not being then known) made Frederick Henrys Bay in 167..55E$^t$ Long$^{de}$ from St Michael, which is 145 degrees East from Greenwich. By dead Reckoning I make Adventure Bay which is on the same Meridian in 140..53 E$^t$ of Greenwich—by good Observations of the Sun & Moon we found it was in 147..45 E, which proves the great utility of Lunar Observations in Long Voyages as without their help I should have made an Error of near 7 degrees in 15 weeks Sailing

[1] Most of the 'Schoutens Islands' to which Burney refers were part of the Freycinet Peninsula. As Tasman indicated on his chart, there is only one Schouten Island which lies off the south of the Peninsula. Tasman had charted the south and east sides of Freycinet Peninsula and some of the coast to the north as part of an island, which he named Vanderlins Eylandt (Van der Lyn's Island).—Sharp, *Voyages of Tasman*, p. 109.

[2] Burney did not realise the irony in his statement. Despite the improvements in navigational techniques since Tasman's voyage, Furneaux's and Burney's misinterpretations of his landmarks and their tendency to see solid land masses as islands resulted in their charts of the east coast of Tasmania being even less accurate than Tasman's.

[3] Burney retained his admiration for Tasman, who had received little praise for his discoveries from the Dutch Government, which was interested in trade rather than exploration. Forty years later in 1813, Burney described Tasman as 'a great and a fortunate Discoverer' and an 'enterprizing and an able navigator' who had 'explored a larger portion of Unknown Sea in a high latitude, and thereby restricted the limits of a supposed Southern Continent, more than any other navigator between the time of Magalhanes [Magellan] and the time of Captain Cook'.—Burney, *Chronological History of Discoveries*, Vol. III, p. 112.

| H. | M. | F. | Courses | Winds | Thursday March 18th |
|---|---|---|---|---|---|
| 1 | 6 | 2 | NWbN | South | A fine fresh Gale. Weather Cloudy— |
| 2 | 6 | 4 | NBW½W | — | running along the Shore at about 4 |
| 3 | 6 | 4 | NbW | — | miles distant at 3/4 past 4 were abrest |
| 4 | 6 | 2 | | | a point which we namd Sᵗ Helens— |
| 5 | 6 | 2 | | | Small, low Rocks run off it for 2 miles |
| 6 | 6 | 2 | | | off Shore—from here the Land falls |
| 7 | 2 | 2 | NbE | | off into a deep Bay which we named |
| | 2 | 2 | NE | | the Bay of Fires, as we saw a great |
| 8 | 4 | 3 | E½N | | many all along the Coast. Northward |
| 9 | 5 | " | | | of this Bay are Rocks which we calld |
| 10 | 4 | " | ESE | | the Eddystone— |
| 11 | 2 | 4 | | | |
| 12 | 2 | 4 | | | |
| 1 | 2 | 4 | | | The Country here affords a very fine |
| 2 | 2 | " | EBS | SBE | prospect. it is low level ground & |
| 3 | 2 | 2 | | | much better inhabited than any part |
| 4 | 2 | " | ESE | South | yet seen by us. So we judge by the |
| 5 | 2 | " | WBS | SBW | fires—at 6 in the Evening Shortend |
| 6 | 3 | 2 | | | Sail—& at ½ past Hauld off Shore |
| 7 | 4 | 2 | | | to the Eastward—the Northernmost |
| 8 | 4 | 4 | | | Land in Sight, which made in 2 |
| 9 | 6 | 2 | NW½N | | high Hammocks bore NWbW¼W— |
| 10 | 6 | " | — | SBE | Variation pr Azimuth this Evening |
| 11 | 6 | " | — | SBE | 8 degrees East—had very strong |
| 12 | 6 | 4 | NNW½W | — | Gales in the Night with Squally |

Weather. at 1 Furld the Topsails—at 4 Wore and made Sail in
Shore—at Sunrise Saw Land bearing N.W. b N. making like 3
Islands. at 8 Saw the High Hammocks which I sett last Night—
find we have been drove a good deal to the Northward in the
Night. we now kept away for the Land to the N.W. at 9 the
Hammocks above mentiond bore S.W. ½ S. from here the Land
turns Short off to the Westward. whether this is a deep Bay, or a
Streight I cant tell, but I think it not at all unlikely that here is a
passage between New Holland & Van demen's Land[1]. The Land

---

[1] The *Adventure* had, in fact, crossed Banks Strait which separates the
Tasmanian mainland from the Furneaux Islands and is an entrance to the
larger strait (Bass Strait) between Tasmania and the Australian continent.
In the latitude of 40°50′S, Furneaux observed 'the Land trenches away to the
westward' but concluded 'it is my opinion that there is no Streights between
New Holland and Van Dieman's Land, but a very deep bay'. As Burney

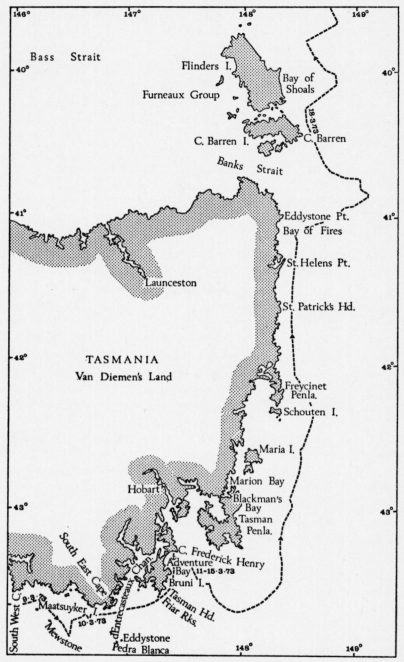

Fig. 2. The east coast of Tasmania.

to the N.W$^t_.$ of us are Islands at 11 were abrest the S.E$^t_.$ End of them. This for its unfruitfull & dreary appearance we calld Cape Barren. there is a low Sandy Island with small Rocks close to it. at Noon the Cape Bore South 1/4 West 6 or 7 miles—Lat$^{de}_.$ Obs$^d$ 40°..21' South Longitude made from Adventure Bay 0°..41' E$^t_.$—

Appearance of Cape Barren bearing S.$\frac{1}{2}$ W. 7 miles—

| H. | M. | F. | Courses | Winds | Friday March 19th 1773— |
|----|----|----|---------|-------|-------------------------|
| 1 | 6 | 4 | North | SSE | A fresh breeze with Cloudy weather |
| 2 | 5 |   | " NEbE |   | at 1 Saw Beaches on the Sarboard |
| 3 | 5 | 4 | N$\frac{1}{2}$E |   | Bow within half a mile of us. hove a |
| 4 | 6 |   | " NWbW |   | cast of the Lead & found ground at |
| 5 | 6 |   | " NW |   | a quarter less 7 fathoms. hauld off |
| 6 | 5 | 6 |   |   | shore & deepend our water to 15 |
| 7 | 3 |   | " NE |   | fathom—at 3 found no ground at 30 |
| 8 | 2 | 4 | E$\frac{1}{2}$S | SbE | fathom. this we calld the Bay of |
| 9 | 2 | 4 |   |   | Shoals. at 6 Sounded Ground at 10 |
| 10 | 2 | 2 |   |   | fathoms Shortend Sail and stood off |
| 11 | 1 | 6 | SEbE | SbW | shore. at $\frac{1}{2}$ past 10 Brought too Main |
|   |   |   |   |   | topsail to the mast— |

indicates, he did not agree with Furneaux's conclusion that Van Diemen's Land was part of New Holland and left a gap on his chart between Cape Barren Island and the northern coast of Van Diemen's Land. On an almost identical chart in his official log, he wrote in the gap 'suposed Streights or Passage'. Burney's view was shared by astronomer William Bayly and midshipman Richard Hergest. However, as Beaglehole states, no one appeared to suspect the existence of a wider strait north of the Furneaux Islands. Cook accepted Furneaux's opinion and abandoned his plan to sail to Van Diemen's Land from New Zealand: 'sence Captain Furneaux hath in a great degree cleared up this point I have given up all thoughts of going thither ...'. As a result of Furneaux's wrong conclusion and Cook's willingness to accept it, Van Diemen's Land was charted as part of New Holland until Bass and Flinders circumnavigated the island in 1798–9.—*Furneaux's Narrative*, in Beaglehole, *Cook Journals*, II, p. 736; *ibid.*, pp. 153 n. 4, 165; J. Burney, *Log*, PRO Adm. 51/4523, chart of east coast of Van Diemen's Land; W. Bayly, *Journal* (Manuscript in Alexander Turnbull Library, Wellington), entries for 18–19 March 1773; R. Hergest, *Journal*, PRO Adm. 51/4522, entry for 19 March 1773.

*H. M. F. Courses  Winds  Friday March 19th 1773*

| | | | | | |
|---|---|---|---|---|---|
| 12 | | | | | |
| 1 | | | | | |
| 2 | } | Up SE off EbS | | | |
| 3 | | | | | |
| 4 | 1 | 5 | West | SSW | |
| 5 | 1 | 6 | SE Gᵈ | 38 fms | |
| 6 | 2 | " | NW | 35 fms | |
| 7 | 4 | " | — | 28 fms | |
| 8 | 5 | " | NWbW | 22 fms | |
| 9 | 3 | 4 | East | SbE | |
| 10 | 3 | " | | | |
| 11 | 4 | 4 | | | |
| 12 | 4 | 4 | | | |

had Soundings all Night from 10 to 53 fathoms depth increasing as we distancd the Shore. brown Sand and broken Shells. at 3 wore and made Sail for the Land. at 4 Sounded 38 fms. Wore Ship at 5 Bore away to the N.W. at 6 Saw the Land bearing W.S.W. distance 10 or 12 Leagues. This is just to the Northward of the Bay of Shoals. Sounded every half hour at 8 finding we shoald our Water very fast as we went to the N.Wᵗ and no Land being in Sight, we hauld off shore and Stood for New Zealand. at 9 Saw Land from the Masthead bearing N.N.W. 12 or 14 Leagues. all the Land we have past since yesterday Noon, from Cape Barren are a parcel of Sandy uninhabited Islands. The Coast is very Shoal and Dangerous. Latᵈᵉ Obsᵈ at Noon 39..20 Sᵒ which is 16 miles North of my Account. Longᵈ from Adventure Bay 1°..05′ Eᵗ from Greenwᶜʰ 148..50 Eᵗ We now Steerd for Captain Cook's Straits which was our place of Rendezvous[1]—a fresh gale from the Southward which continued till the 28th when it came round to the Northward—

April 2ᵈ we now judge ourselves not far from the Land. in the Night the Wind came round to the S.S.E., blowing very Strong with a great deal of rain—at 4 in the Morning it being quite dark we Shortend Sail. & at daylight we saw the Land bearing E.½ N. distant 3 or 4 Leagues—this proved to be Rock's point in New Zealand. as we drew in with the Land the weather cleard up— at Noon had a pleasant Light breeze with fair Weather—Rocks point bore S.b E.½ E. & Cape Farewell which is in the Mouth of Cook's Straits[2] E.B N.½ N.—Latitude observd 40°..40′ Sᵒ

---

[1] Having concluded that Van Diemen's Land was part of New Holland, Furneaux decided not to sail farther north because of the dangerous shoals and stormy weather. It was 'more prudent', he thought, 'to leave the Coast and steer for New Zealand'.—Furneaux's *Narrative*, in Beaglehole, *Cook Journals*, II, p. 736.

[2] Cook Strait.

Longitude pr dead Reckoning from Adventure Bay—24..49 E?
Long$^{de}$ from Greenw$^{ch}$ by Lunar Observations 172°:04' E.

April 3$^d$ by sunset were abrest Cape Farewell—at ½ past 11
Backd the Maintopsail & Lay too—till ½ past 4 in the Morning
had Soundings all Night from 45 to 58 fms. our distance off
Shore being about 8 Leagues—

Sunday 4$^{th}$ At Noon Stephen's Island bore S.E. 5 or 6 Leagues
Lat$^{de}$ Obs$^d$ 40..17 S? Long$^{de}$ from Greenwich by Lunar Observations 173..16 E$^t$

Monday 5$^{th}$ were this morning off Admiralty Bay—at ½ past 10
Sounded, had ground at 36 fms fine Sand—Point Jackson which
is the West Point of Charlotte Sound bearing S.E? ¼ S—and
Cape Stephens W.N.W.—at ½ past 2 in the afternoon—the Wind
being foul & tide against us, we came to an Anchor between
Admiralty Bay & Charlotte Sound in 39 fathoms a muddy Bottom
—Stephen's Island N.W. & P$^t$ Jackson S.E.½ E. Slack water at
½ past 7 this Evening—at 8 Weighd at Midnight Point Jackson
S.S.E., had no ground at 70 fms—being 5 or 6 miles from the
Shore—next Morning we Anchord in the Outer part of Q.
Charlotte's Sound—in the Afternoon we Weighd the Anchor &
went farther up the Sound & moord the Ship off of Ship Cove—
I was sent this Evening in the Small Cutter to look round the
Cove for a Watering place & to see if there were any marks of the
Resolution having been here—found several very convenient
Watering places with Excellent Water, & one where we judge
Captain Cook Waterd in the Endeavour[1]—the Names of Several
of his people being cut in the Trees. but no Signs of the Resolution[2]
—Caught a great many Fish tonight & Shot some Shelldrakes,
Curlieus & other Birds—which we found here in great plenty—

April 7th have seen no inhabitants as yet, nor signs of any—
there are a great many empty houses in every beach along shore
& some deserted towns. one of them is on a small Isl$^d$ calld the
Hippa. & seems designd for a strong hold—the shore is so steep

---

[1] Cook had spent three weeks at Ship Cove in Queen Charlotte Sound in
January-February 1770 on his first voyage. It became one of his favourite
harbours.
[2] The *Resolution* had arrived at Dusky Sound on the south-west tip of New
Zealand's South Island on 26 March. It did not join the *Adventure* at Queen
Charlotte Sound until 18 May, six weeks after Furneaux's arrival.

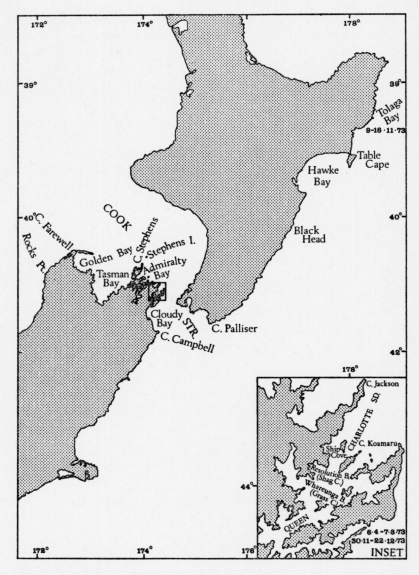

Fig. 3. Parts of New Zealand visited by the *Resolution* and *Adventure*.

that it is almost inaccessible except at one place & that none of the Easiest. at the top is a wall about 5 feet high made of brambles between 2 Rows of Stakes—very neat. on this spot our Astronomer fixed his observatory—When Capt. Cook was here in the Endeavour the Hyppa was inhabited[1]; This Island lays close to another, much larger calld the Motuara in C. Cooks Chart—on this we erected a Tent for the convenience of repairing our Sails, Casks &c & getting the Sick on shore—5 in number & only one of the scurvy—we have been all very hearty thank God, since we left the Cape.[2] we now employd ourselves in repairing our Rigging, wooding, Watering & other necessary things—This Night we heard the Voices of men & the barking of dogs—

April 9th. Some Canoes came down the Sound—2 of them a double\* one & a single one came to the Ship—at about 20 yards distance they stopd Short when one of them Stood up & made a long Speech, every now & then waving a Bough, the rest keeping a profound Silence—after this they ventured alongside & came on board. They enquired for Tobia (the man C. Cook brought from Otaheite)—were much concernd at hearing he was dead & seemed to suspect we had put him to death, till we made Signs that the Almighty had killd him[3]—we made them several presents & bought some of their Arms & Cloaths—they began to be very familiar till by chance one of our Gentlemen saw a human head in one of the Canoes—wrapt up in a Hahoo (the name of their cloth)[4]—on our discovering this, they all got out of

---

[1] Beaglehole, *Cook Journals*, I, p. 239.

[2] Cf. Furneaux who states that the *Adventure* had 'several onboard much inflicted with the Scurvy' on arrival at Queen Charlotte Sound.—*Furneaux's Narrative*, in Beaglehole, *Cook Journals*, II, p. 737.

[3] Tobia (Tupaia) had been taken on board the *Endeavour* at Tahiti in July 1769 on Cook's first voyage. His patron was Joseph Banks who wrote in his journal: 'I do not know why I may not keep him as a curiosity, as well as some of my neighbours do lions and tygers at a larger expence than he will probably ever put me to . . .'. Tobia proved useful because of his knowledge of the Society Islands, and, more particularly, because he was able to communicate with the Maoris in New Zealand. To Banks's disappointment, Tobia did not survive the homeward voyage. Weakened by scurvy, he developed a fever and died while the ships were at Batavia.—Beaglehole, *Endeavour Journal*, I, pp. 312–13; II, pp. 190–1; Beaglehole, *Cook Journals*, I, pp. 169, 240, 427, 441–2.

[4] *kahu*: a general term for a Maori cloak. See p. 52 and p. 52 n. 1.

\* *double Canoes are 2 fastend together by sticks that go across them. by this means they are not in danger of oversetting, which the single ones do, as I have experienced*

the ship & although many of us tried hard to get a sight of it afterwards, as we thought the person that saw it might be mistaken, we could not satisfy ourselves without we had used force which we did not choose to do. Nethertheless they were so much offended, or frightend with our having seen it that they went away as fast as they could.[2] the next day however 5 Canoes came on board, they took no notice of what had passed, but were very free & friendly—

Sunday 11th it blew too fresh to day for the Indians to come on board. This afternoon we cleard a spot of ground for a Garden & Set several kinds of seeds—Sow'd pease & Wheat all which came up to great perfection in a Short time—

Monday 12th More Canoes came down the Sound—we had 10 alongside of us—at Night they all went up the Harbour together on account of bad weather which they said was coming— they were not mistaken—we saw no more of them till the middle of the next week—

April 21st this morning the Captn sent the Large Cutter up the Sound with the Master & acting Lieutenant. in the afternoon 3 small Canoes came to the Ship & remaind in Ship Cove till the 25th supplying us every day with fish, of which the Captain for 3 or 4 nails would purchase a sufficient quantity to serve the whole Ships Company. we seldom had occasion for their fish as we caught great plenty ourselves—but we always bought them that they might be encouraged to come often—

April 22d at Noon the Cutter returned having been 7 Leagues up without seeing any Inhabitants or being able to find where the Sound ends. further up it inclines more to the westward, which makes one imagine it runs into Admiralty Bay—it is not improbable that Cape Koamaroo, Point Jackson, & all the broken land hereabouts are Seperate Islands & that there is

---

[1] The Maoris knew that the Europeans abhorred their cannibalism and, as Burney indicates, tried to conceal the human head. Cook had received visual proof of the Maoris' admission that they ate their enemies when, in January 1770 on his first voyage, he found the bones and other remains of some recently eaten bodies at Queen Charlotte Sound.—Beaglehole, *Cook Journals*, I, pp. 236–7.

a communication at the back, all the way from Cloudy Bay to Blind Bay[1]—either Admiralty Bay or Cloudy Bay must be the same which Tasman calls Murderers Bay on account of his losing 3 men there[2]—

Sunday 25th. This day we hove our Anchors up & got further into Ship Cove being too much exposed to the S.S.W. wind which sometimes blows very Strong down the sound—In the afternoon 2 large Canoes with about 30 Indians came to our Tent from the Northward—these are the first we have seen from that quarter— on the 28th we Shifted our Tent from the Island to the Watering place in the Cove, it being nearer the ship & more convenient—

May—All our occurrences for the first half of this Month is but a repetition of the Old Story—the Zealanders now & then came down the Sound, Staid 2 or 3 days and went back again—we have not had more than 3 Canoes with us at a time since the first week of our coming here—The New Zealanders are a Stout well made people very active, knowing & undoubtedly capable of great improvement—but they are at present in a state very little, if anything, superior to the Brute part of the Creation— being Cannibals, many of them Thieves & cursed lousy. yet I must do them the Justice to acknowledge the two last mentioned qualities are not general—some being very cleanly & I believe honest. as to the other part of the Story I have not much to say in their behalf—I am apt to think they eat their prisoners—this may in a great measure be owing to their poor manner of living & not knowing how to make the most of what they have—we have seen no quadrupeds here except dogs & not many of them. They live mostly on fish which are in great plenty—they have

---

[1] Burney was wrong. There was no passage from Cloudy Bay to Blind Bay (now Tasman Bay). Cook later made a similar, though less serious, error when he thought that Blind Bay might be connected at least to Queen Charlotte Sound.—Beaglehole, *Cook Journals*, II, p. 142.

[2] Burney was wrong again. Tasman's Murderers Bay (now Golden Bay) was farther west, immediately east of Cape Farewell. Cook identified it correctly on 18 May 1773 when he was en route from Dusky Bay to Queen Charlotte Sound: 'about Six leagues to the Eastward of Cape Farewell there seems to be a spacious Bay covered from the Sea by a low point of land and is I beleive the same as Tasman first anchored in'. Tasman had named the bay Murderers Bay on 19 December 1642 after a group of Maoris attacked the *Zeehaen's* cockboat, killing three men and fatally wounding a fourth.— Beaglehole, *Cook Journals*, II, p. 142; Sharp, *Voyages of Tasman*, pp. 121-4.

Some method of catching fowls, but I believe more then 6 days out of 7 they get nothing but fish. they roast & bake all their Victuals having no vessels that will bear the fire—Fern Roots serves them for Bread—their people are not naturally cruel or wanting in Social affections—I have frequently seen them Shed tears at parting, which they never do if only for an hour without joining noses. (their manner of saluting)—towards us they behaved very friendly & endeavoured to make us believe they were fond of us, I will not pretend to determine whether this was out of love, fear, or for what they could get—they are not negligent of their interest when anything is to be got, this we have had proof of— but as to fear either they are very little acquainted with it or must have a very good opinion of us, otherwise they would not have put themselves so much in our power as they have—nevertheless I don't think it prudent to trust them too far—

Their Dress is a Square piece of Cloth of their own manufacture (of Flax) calld Hahoo, this is wrapd round them and fastened with a belt. They have a kind of a matt which they call Buggy, that they wear over the Hahoo in bad weather—they wear nothing on their head or feet—their hair is commonly tied up on the crown of their head in which they Stick feathers & Combs made of fish bones.[1] They have pieces of green jasper[2] & rows of teeth in their Ears—The women dress the same as the men— some of them paint their faces red & the greater part of both sexes have one lip staind blue. some of the men have their faces prickd & staind in very curious flourishes; this custom is calld Tattow. I imagine it is a mark of honour which those only are entitled to who have done something extraordinary. Some are tattowd only on one Side & some all over the face—those who are thus distinguished are greatly respected by the rest, especially those who are tattowd both sides—

They likewise scarify their Arms & foreheads when any of their friends or Relations die. as to their notion of another world none of us could ever discover anything about it—that they have a Religion of some kind I don't in the least doubt—

These people differ greatly in their colour, some being almost white some olive & some quite black—the Arms the Zealanders

---

[1] *kahu; paakee.* The various types of *kahu* and *paakee* are described by S.M. Mead, *Traditional Maori Clothing* (Wellington, 1969), pp. 47–63, 222–3.

[2] Greenstone (nephrite). Greenstone is not a form of jasper.

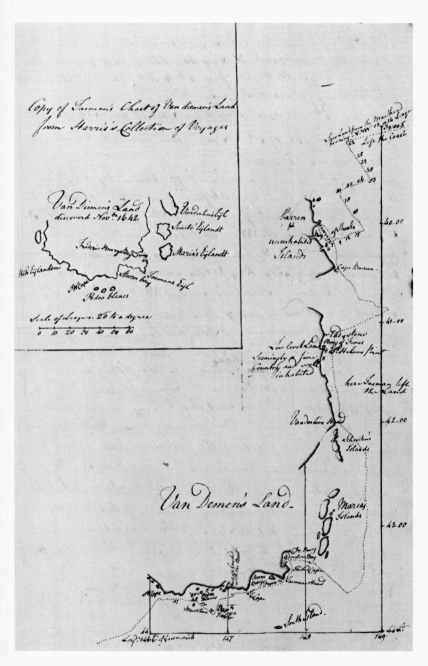

Plate 3. Burney's chart of Tasmania's east coast.

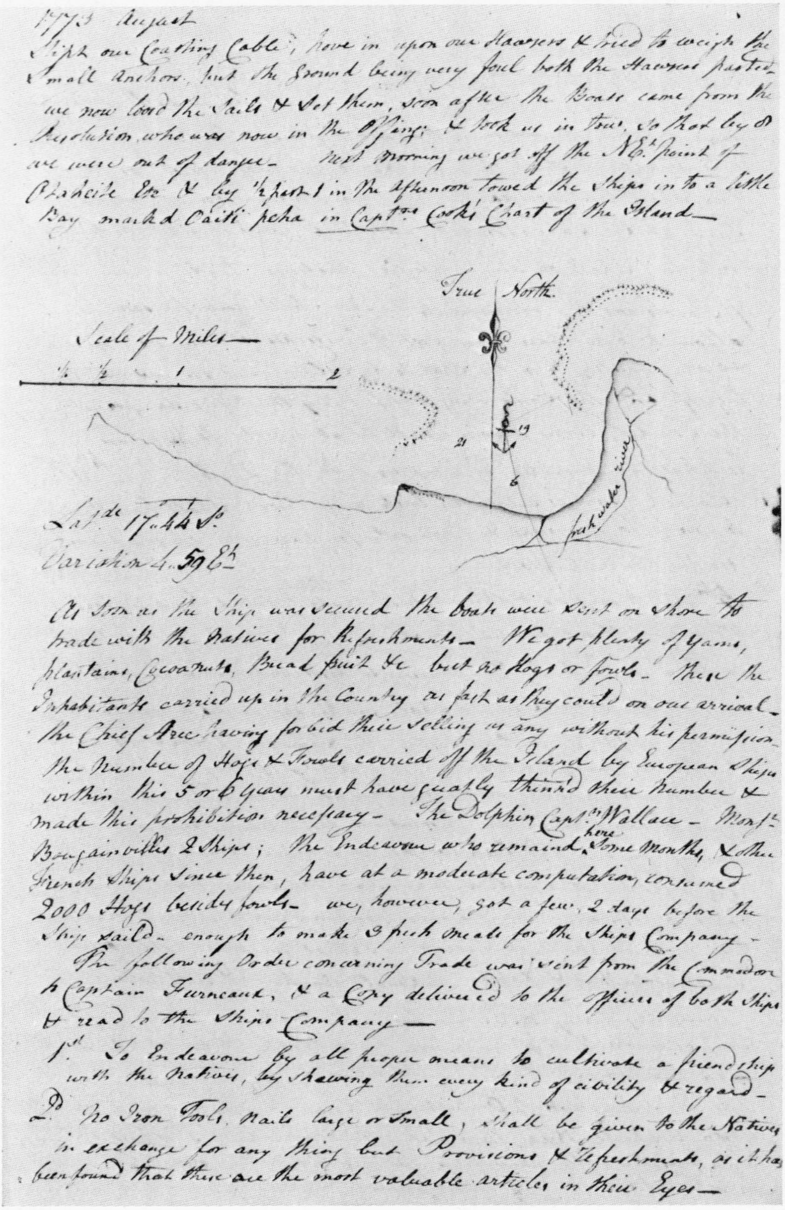

1773 August

Slipt our Coasting Cable, hove in upon our Hawsers & tried to weigh the small anchors, but the Ground being very foul both the Hawsers parted — we now loos'd the Sails & set them, soon after the Boats came from the Resolution who were now in the Offing & took us in tow, so that by 8 we were out of danger — Next morning we got off the N.E. point of Otahicite &c & by [report] in the afternoon towed the Ships into a little Bay marked Oaiti peha in Captⁿ Cooks Chart of the Island —

True North

Scale of Miles

Latde 17° 44′ Sᵗ
Variation 4° 59′ Eᵗ

As soon as the Ships was secured the boats were sent on shore to trade with the Natives for Refreshments — We got plenty of Yams, plantains, Cocoanuts, Bread fruit &c but no Hogs or fowls — these the Inhabitants carried up in the Country as fast as they could on our arrival — the Chief Aree having forbid their selling us any without his permission — the Number of Hogs & Fowls carried off the Island by European Ships within this 5 or 6 years must have greatly thinn'd their number & made this prohibition necessary — The Dolphin Captⁿ Wallace — Monsⁱᵉʳ Bougainvilles 2 Ships; the Endeavour who remaind here some months, & other French Ships since then, have at a moderate computation consumed 2000 Hogs besides fowls — we, however, got a few, 2 days before the Ships sail'd — enough to make 3 fresh meals for the Ships Company —

The following Order concerning Trade was sent from the Commodore to Captain Furneaux, & a Copy delivered to the Officers of both Ships & read to the Ships Company —

1ˢᵗ To Endeavour by all proper means to cultivate a friendship with the Natives, by shewing them every kind of civility & regard —

2ᵈ No Iron Tools, Nails large or small, shall be given to the Natives in exchange for any thing but Provisions & Refreshments, as it has been found that these are the most valuable articles in their Eyes —

Plate 4. A page from the journal,
with Burney's drawing of Vaitepiha Bay, Tahiti.

use are Clubs & Spears. The Club (I dont know their name for it) is 6 or 7 feet long made of very hard heavy wood. The End is flat, not much unlike the blade of an oar making 2 Edges, not sharp—there is no occasion, the weight would be sufficient to do any mans business.[1]

Their Spears (calld by them Hepatoo) are some of them 26 feet long—Sharp pointed, some at both ends.[2] They dont dart these but use them as we do pikes or fixed bayonets—besides these 2 they have another weapon which they use when too near for anything else. it is shaped like a battledore much about the same size—they are made either of stone, hard wood or Bone. This they call the patow.[3] I have wonder'd at their not having Bows & Arrows, as they are in use at all the Islands, I have ever heard of, in the South Seas. These people are not so fond of Trifles & Toys as one might expect—they look out for the Main chance & know very well what is usefull. all the Beads & Trinkets we gave them they did not value so much as a large Spike Nail or a Hatchet—a gimblet or a quart bottle will go a great way with them—the Tools they work with are made of Stone, many of a kind of green jasper which they call poenamoo[4]—They are very clean & neat in their work—their houses are very little better than Huts being not more than 5 or 6 feet high with a small door. that you must creep in on all fours—but they are warm & both wind & water tight—

Of all the Customs peculiar to these people their Heavoh[5] or War Dance seems to me the most remarkable & is the most difficult to describe—they all get in a Row & jump & put themselves in many different strange attitudes, sometimes rolling their eyes about frightfully—one of them speaks a number of Short Sentences, at every one of which they change their posture, keeping exact time & very regularly through all their motions—they have another dance where one sings or speaks, laying a

[1] *tewhatewha*: one of several types of long two-handed wooden clubs used by the Maoris. Elsdon Best, *The Maori* (2 vols. Wellington, 1924), Vol. II, pp. 251–3.

[2] Best, *The Maori*, Vol. II, pp. 240–5, lists sixteen types of thrusting spear but does not include one with this name.

[3] *patu*: the generic term for single-handed clubs. For descriptions of some of the Maori weapons collected by Cook on his first voyage, see Wilfred Shaw-cross, 'The Cambridge University Collection of Maori Artefacts, made on Captain Cook's First Voyage', *Journal of the Polynesian Society*, 79 (1970), pp. 312–20.

[4] *pounamu*: greenstone.

[5] *heiva*.

particular stress on every third or fourth syllable—or rather jerking it out—this is accompanied by the rest with a jump, & a noise a good deal resembling the grunting of a hog—

The whole Country in this Southern Island is a continued ridge of hills throughout & quite overrun with wood. the Vallies are well waterd & the Soil, So I am told, is excellent—for I am no judge of it myself—Our Garden is in a flourishing Condition— every thing we have set shoots up but the Rats play the devel with our pease—here is plenty of Wild Cellery, Scurvy grass & other greens very good for boiling—but the Indians make no use of them. Here are 2 trees with fruit—one of them bears berries about the Size of our plumbs but not to be compared with them for goodness; when ripe they are between red & yellow—the other which is the largest Tree bears small red berries about the same Size as the seed of a Pomegranate & not much unlike them in flavour[1]—we are now clearing a piece of ground for another garden—

May 10th at ¼ past 5 this afternoon we felt 2 Slight shocks of an Earthquake—

Tuesday 18th This morning at Sunrise we were alarmed by 2 Musquetoons being fired at the Astronomers Tent on the Hippa— which we soon found to our great joy & satisfaction, was meant as a signal for the Resolution who was then coming in round Point Jackson. We sent our Cutter to her with fish & Sallad from the garden & it afterwards falling little wind we sent our Launch with an Anchor & Hawser to assist her, if necessary— in the evening she anchord in the Cove within a quarter of a mile of us. Our satisfaction was not a little increased at finding them all well & hearty[2]—After we parted they cruis'd about for

---

[1] Probably the *karaka* (*Corynocarpus laevigata*) and the *kahikatea* (*Podocarpus dacrydioides*), both of which bear fruit in the autumn. Joseph Banks had not been impressed with the local fruit when he visited New Zealand from October 1769 to March 1770 on Cook's first voyage. He wrote in his journal: 'Fruits they have none, except I should reckon a few kind of insipid berries which had neither sweetness nor flavour to recommend them . . .'.—Leonard Cockayne, *The Vegetation of New Zealand*, third ed. (Weinheim/Bergstr., 1958), pp. 66–7, 122; Beaglehole, *Endeavour Journal*, II, p. 9.

[2] Cook made prodigious efforts to keep his men free from scurvy, giving them fresh vegetables at every possible opportunity. At Dusky Sound, where there were no vegetables, he brewed beer using the leaves and branches of the Rimu tree, wort (infusion of malt) and molasses. As soon as he arrived at

us 3 days, firing guns & burning false fires at their main topmast head every hour in the Night. but finding it to no purpose & being unwilling to lose any more of a fair wind they bore away to the S.S.E$^t$ & recruited their Stock of Water again amongst the Ice, going into 63° S? they afterwards hauld up for Van Diemens Land but were too far to the S?ward to fetch it, the Wind blowing constantly from the N.W. by the latter end of March they got into Dusky Bay near the South Cape of New Zealand where they remained 6 weeks & then came here.

By the End of this Month we were ready for sea[1]—this fortnight past have seen very little of the Indians. Capt$^n$ Cook & Capt$^n$ Furneaux have clear'd a large piece of ground & Sowd Wheat in it—

June. Tuesday 1$^{st}$ this day several Canoes with Sails made of mats came down the Sound to us—the next day the Captains carried an Old Indian to the field of wheat & to the Gardens, recommending them to his Care & endeavourd to make him sensible it was their interest not to destroy them.[2] the Old Man seemd to know something of the Matter & staid a good while in the garden picking the Stones out of the Beds—we now got our Tent & all the Lumber on board—

2$^d$ This Evening whilst our boat was ashore in a little bay where the Indians lived for the convenience of coming to us, 2 of them had very high words & not being able to accomodate matters amicably, they both strippd naked, took each of them a stick & beat one another till one gave out, none of the rest interfering all the time—the Indians next morning told us they afterwards

---

Queen Charlotte Sound, he and his men gathered celery, scurvy grass and other local vegetables which he ordered to be served daily for breakfast and dinner. Cook took care to ensure that his order 'was punctualy complied with at least in [his] sloop', suspecting that Furneaux was not so insistent.— Beaglehole, *Cook Journals*, II, pp. 114, 165–8.

[1] Furneaux was prepared to winter in Queen Charlotte Sound but Cook, who did not want to 'Idle away the whole Winter in Port', proposed 'exploring the unknown parts of the Sea to the East and North'. Cook had abandoned his earlier intention of visiting Van Diemen's Land. (see note p. 43).—Beaglehole, *Cook Journals*, II, p. 165.

[2] Cook had enlarged the area of garden planted by Furneaux. When Burney returned to Queen Charlotte Sound in February 1777 on Cook's third voyage, he found the gardens were 'so overrun with weeds and underwood that we could scarcely distinguish the remains'.—Beaglehole, *Cook Journals*, II, p. 169; Burney, *Journal*, PRO Adm. 51/4528, entry for 13 February 1777.

fought with their Clubs or Battle Axes & one of them was killed in the battle.

3ᵈ All the Canoes except 3 Small ones with about 20 Indians went up the Sound this Afternoon we put a Hog & 2 Sows (one of them with Pig) on shore in an unfrequented place—if the Zealanders do not find them out & destroy them there may be a fine breed in a Short time—but its ten to one if they are not hunted down soon after we go away.[1] As yet I have not mentioned their Music. I shall say but little on this subject for very little will suffice. their Instruments are Flutes & Trumpets—the flutes are more curious for their carving than for any music that can be got out of them. I shall bring home a Specimen. the Trumpet is a Tube about 7 feet long—they make these & the flutes by getting a piece of wood fit for their purpose. They then shape it on the outside & afterwoods split it in 2. These parts being hollowd are woulded [sic] together & are sure to fit exactly. I saw but one of their Trumpets the whole time we staid here & that Captⁿ Furneaux got—the notes on this vary according as you blow more or less. I question whether a man who understands the French horn might not be able to play a Tune on it—as to the Zealanders they constantly sounded the same Note. Tasman mentions one of these Instruments in his account of Murderers Bay[2]—

The Zealanders commonly give us a Song when they leave the Ship—there is no great variety in the Music, however it comes nearer to a Tune than anything I have heard here—the words I neither understood nor can remember—here is the Tune they

[1] In addition to the animals put ashore by Furneaux, Cook left sheep, pigs and goats. A ewe and a ram which he 'had with so much care and trouble' taken to New Zealand died soon after they were put ashore. Cook still hoped that the country would be eventually stocked with goats and hogs and thought there was 'no great danger that the Natives will destroy them as they are exceedingly afraid of both'. Burney's less optimistic forecast proved correct. When Cook returned to Queen Charlotte Sound on his third voyage, he was informed that the animals 'were all dead'.—Beaglehole, *Cook Journals*, II, pp. 166–9; III, p. 67.

[2] On 18 December 1642, Tasman reported that the natives 'blew also many times on an Instrument which gave sound like the Moors' Trumpets'.—Sharp, *Voyages of Tasman*, p. 121. Peter Buck, *The Coming of the Maori*, second ed. (Wellington, 1950), pp. 257–67, discusses the various types of trumpets and flutes used by the Maoris. Some of the Maori musical instruments collected by Cook on his first voyage are described in detail by Shawcross, *Journal of the Polynesian Society*, 79, pp. 334–8.

keep singing the 2 first Bars till their words are expended & then close with the last—Sometimes they Sing an underpart which is a third lower except the 2 last notes which are the same[1]—

June 4th this Morning a large double Canoe with about 36 people (all men) came to the Resolution from the Motuara Island —these are Strangers that we have never seen before—I believe they came from the N.E[t] or from East Bay in the Night & went to the Island for a Lodging – before they ventured along side one of their Chiefs made a most unconscionable long Oration & was answered by some of the Southern Indians that were on board the Resolution. These at first were much frighten'd & wanted Capt[n] Cook to shoot the New Comers—but after they were on board, he made them join Noses, after which they were very good friends & some of the Southern Indians went over to the Island with them. These Indians seem much Superior to any we have yet seen here—being stouter, better drest, & having better Canoes & Arms than our Old Acquaintances—There were 2 Chiefs amongst them, each Tattowd on both sides of the face— one was a very stout old man who might have stood to a Statuary for the Model of a Hercules—he was dressd in black dog's skins very curiously workd into a Hahoo. The other Chief was a young man who wore a very fine striped Hahoo which the Commodore purchased. when the Indians went back to the Island the Commodore followed them in his pinnace & found 5 Canoes with about 100 people (men women & children)[2]—

This being His Majestys Birthday the Officers of both Ships were invited to dine with the Commodore & we had a very jovial Afternoon. The 2 following days it blew very fresh from the Southward with dirty weather—on the 7th early in the morning the weather being more moderate, we hove up our Anchor & made Sail out of Q.Charlottes Sound, which is without exception, one of the finest havens in the World. Point Jackson which is the

[1] Cook thought the Maoris' songs were 'harmonious enough but very dolefull to a European Ear'.—Beaglehole, *Cook Journals*, I, p. 285.
[2] See Beaglehole, *Cook Journals*, II, pp. 171–2.

N.W. point of the Sound lyes in 40..58 S? Latitude & in 174° E?
Longitude from the Meridian of Greenwich. Variation 14..05 E?
in the year 1642 Tasman found it 9 degrees East. the Tide here
rises about 6 feet perpendicular—High water on the full &
Change at 9 hours.

June 7th all this afternoon we were turning to windward to get
through Cooks Straits the wind being from the Southward—
in the Evening the wind Shifted & on the Noon of the 8th we
took our departure from C.Pallisser[1] which is the Southernmost
point of North Zealand. Latitude 41°..36' S° & Longde 174..
54 E? from Greenwch We now Stand to the E.S.E. till we got
into 47°½S? Latde but bad weather coming on we Slanted to the
Northward again & kept nearly in the parallel of 43° till the
middle of July nothing material happening. having gone 50
degrees of Longde East of New Zealand without the least Appearance of Land. We now stood to the Northward to get into the
Trade wind, which we expected to find in 25 or 26° South

July 27th this day Our Cook (who had been a long time bad)
died of a complication of distempus
   The Winds continuing between the North & N.W. points of the
Compass hindered us from running our Latitude down as fast as
we expected, & obliged us to go more to the Eastward which
increasd our distance from Otaheite, the place of our destination—
what made this of consequence was, our people began to fall sick,
the flux and the Scurvy made its appearance amongst us & the
Sick list daily increased—we did not get the Trade Wind till
the Night of the 6th of August, being then in 19°½ South Latitude
& 227 ½ E? Longde from Greenwich. the Number of Sick has
increased to 28 who are all unable to do duty—this is more than a
third of the Ship's Company. the Resolution people are all in
good health & hearty—Our Sickness is, l believe chiefly owing to
our Ships being greatly Lumber'd the people have scarce room
to stir below—& this is more sensibly felt, coming from a cold
climate to a hot one—our tedious passage has greatly contributed
to depress their spirits, especially as this was proposed when we

---

[1] Cape Palliser.

left New Zealand as a Cruize for refreshment.[1] But the Trade Wind will, I hope be a good Doctor, & Otaheite an excellent Medicine Chest that will set us all to rights again—One of the Resolution's gentlemen says nothing hurts him more than this Cruize being mentioned as a party of pleasure, if, says he, they had put it down to the account of hard services, I had been content & thought myself well off, but to have it set down under the Article of Refreshment is d——d hard.

August 11th at ½ past 6 this morning Saw Land bearing S.S.W. dis[t] 7 or 8 miles—This proved to be 2 or 3 Small low Islands not extending more than 3 or 4 miles any way—there seems to be plenty of Palm & Cocoanut trees on them. we were not near enough to know if they were inhabited.[2]

Thursday 12th at daylight this morning Saw another Small group of Islands with a Reef running all round the S.E. & South Side of them—these are very little larger than those we saw yesterday & afford much the same prospect—we ran 7 or 8 miles along the Reef & after 8 saw nothing of them. Small as these Islands are they are not without inhabitants—we saw a Canoe within the Reef with 4 Indians in it. These Islands lay in 17..06 S[o] Lat[de]. & in 217° ½ E[t] Longitude. those we saw yesterday in 17°..24′ S° & 218°..53′ E—the two small Reefs obliged us to lay too every night or send a boat before us with a light—on Sunday

---

[1] As Burney states, there was a marked difference in the health of the men on board the two ships. The *Resolution* had only one man suffering from scurvy. When others began showing signs of the illness, Cook put them on a diet of 'Wort, Marmalade of Carrots, Rob of Lemons and Oranges'. In response to his suggestion that similar measures should be taken on board the *Adventure*, Furneaux claimed that he had already 'tried all the remedies that could be invented' and that the only one to have had any effect was wort 'which if it did not cure prevented [the men] from growing worse'. When Cook attempted to account for the difference in the state of health in the two ships, he made no mention of Burney's contention that the illness on board the *Adventure* was due to overcrowding. Instead, he attributed it to the *Adventure's* men 'being more Scorbutic when they arrived in New-Zealand' and their having eaten 'few or no Vegetables while they lay in Queen Charlottes Sound'. Cook insinuated that Furneaux had not been sufficiently insistent on his men eating fresh vegetables, stating that 'both the example and Authority of a Commander' were necessary to overcome the prejudices of seamen and make them eat celery and scurvy grass.—Beaglehole, *Cook Journals*, II, pp. 187, 191 n. 2; see also notes p. 60 n.3 and p. 64 n.2.

[2] The ships were passing through the Tuamotu Archipelago, east of Tahiti.

the 15th we saw Osnaburg[1] Island & in the afternoon saw Otaheite[2] bearing W. ½ S. 14 or 16 Leagues distant at Night we lay too & in the morning got close in with the Land—a great many Canoes came off to us with Cocoanuts, Plantains &c of which we got plenty for the people. this forenoon we got our boats out & sent to the Resolution for assistance. Capt^n. Cook sent us 13 men who remained with us till the Ship was secured[3]—

I must now copy my Log for the Remainder of this day & the forenoon of the 17^th.—

16^th at Noon the Exrtemes of Otaheite* Ete from N.W. to South dist^t. off shore about half a League. Lat^de. Obs^d 17°..46′ S°. Light Airs from the Eastward with fair Weather. at 2 this afternoon the Resolution being very near the Reef that surrounds this part of the Island, Sent our boats to assist her—having but little wind & that on Shore, with a strong Indraught the Resolution was obliged to come to an Anchor as were we likewise at the same time close by her & luckely got ground at 20 fathoms with our Coasting anchor Veerd away to almost half a Cable which brought us up—carried out a Kedge Anchor & 3 Hawsers which we let go in 55 fathoms—Hauld the Ship further out & sent the boats with another Kedge Anchor & 2 Hawsers more out which was let go in above 90 fms—in the mean time there being an opening in the Reef, Capt^n. Cook sent a boat to see if there was depth of water sufficient for the Ships to get within the Reef, but found no more than 12 feet depth—We hoisted out our Launch & sent her to weigh our Coasting Anchor, but were prevented by all the boats being wanted to tow the Resolution off, She having Struck several times. it being now quite calm they got her out—at ½ past 5 a light air Springing up from the S.S.W. we Shipt our Coasting Cable, hove in upon our Hawsers & tried to weigh the Small Anchor, but the ground being very foul both the Hawsers parted—we now loosd the Sails & set them, soon after the Boats came

---

[1] Now Mehetia.

[2] Tahiti. Early European visitors to Tahiti thought that the prefix 'O' (it is) was part of the name of the island.

[3] According to Furneaux, the *Adventure* had '30 Men in the Sick List with the Scurvy and but few others without Scorbutic complaints'. In contrast, Cook still reported 'only one Scorbutic person' on board the *Resolution*.— Furneaux, *Journal*, PRO Adm. 55/1, entry for 16 August 1773; Beaglehole, *Cook Journals*, II, p. 205.

* *Otaheite is divided into 2 parts joined by a low Isthmus–Ete signifies little.*

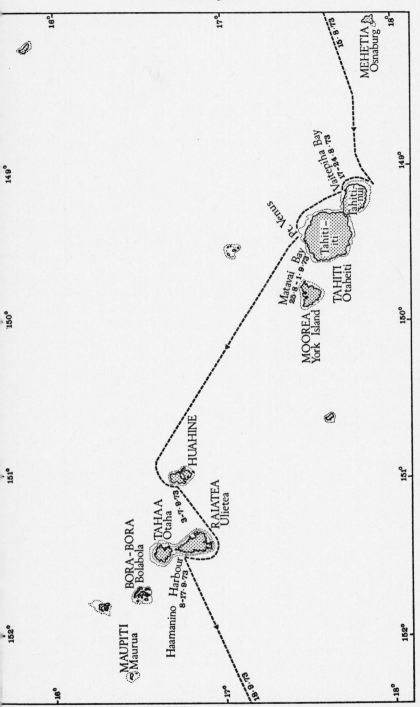

Fig. 4. The Society Islands.

from the Resolution, who was now in the Offing; & took us in tow, so that by 8 we were out of danger[1]—Next Morning we got off the N.E.ᵗ point of Otaheite Ete & by ½ past 1 in the Afternoon towed the Ships in to a little Bay. marked Oaiti peha[2] in Captⁿ. Cook's Chart of the Island—

As Soon as the Ship was secured the Boats were sent on shore to trade with the Natives for Refreshments—We got plenty of yams, plantains, Cocoanuts, Bread fruit &c but no Hogs or fowls—these the Inhabitants carried up in the Country as fast as they could on our arrival—the Chief Aree[3] having forbid their selling us any without his permission the number of Hogs & fowls carried off the Island by European Ships within this 5 or 6 years must have greatly thinnd their number & made this prohibition necessary—The Dolphin Captⁿ. Wallace—Monsʳ Bougainvilles 2 Ships; the Endeavour who remaind here some months, & other French Ships since then[4], have at a moderate computation, consumed 2000 Hogs besides fowls—we, however, got a few, 2 days before the Ships saild—enough to make 3 fresh meals for the Ships Company—

The following Order concerning Trade was sent from the Commodore & Captain Furneaux, & a Copy delivered to the officers of both Ships & read to the Ships Company—

1ˢᵗ. To Endeavour by all proper means to cultivate a friendship with the Natives, by showing them every kind of civility & regard—

2ᵈ. No Iron Tools, Nails large or Small, shall be given to the

---

[1] In his haste to reach Tahiti to obtain fresh provisions, Cook had approached the island on the south-east side, exposing the ships to both a strong tide and a reef. When they were unable to find a passage through the reef, the ships were carried towards it by the tide. While Burney was able to describe the narrow escape from shipwreck unemotionally, Cook had vivid memories of the *Endeavour's* near destruction on the Great Barrier Reef in June 1770 and expressed great relief when they were finally safe 'after a narrow escape of being Wrecked on the very Island we but a few days ago so ardently wished to be at'.—Beaglehole, *Cook Journals*, II, pp. 199–200.

[2] Vaitepiha Bay.

[3] *arii*. See p. 69 n. 5.

[4] The first known European visit to Tahiti was made in 1767 when the *Dolphin*, captained by Samuel Wallis, spent over a month at the island. The French explorer Louis Antoine de Bougainville called there in 1768 and, a year later, James Cook spent three months at Tahiti where he observed the transit of Venus. No French ship had been to Tahiti since Bougainville's visit. Burney was probably referring to the Spanish ship, the *Aguila*, commanded by Don Domingo de Boenechea, which visited Tahiti in November–December 1772.

Natives in exchange for any thing but Provisions & Refreshments, as it has been found that these are the most valuable articles in their Eyes[1]—

Art.3$^{\underline{d}}$ The Exchanges on board, or alongside, the Ship, or at the Publick Market Place on shore (if any) Shall be under the inspection of one or more Commission or Warrant Officers, who shall from time to time appoint such other persons to trade or assist, as he or they shall find necessary—And no other Person or Persons but such as are so appointed and those comprehended in the 4$^{th}$ Article, Shall on any pretence whatever trade for any kind of Provisions & Refreshments: Nor shall any person be allowed to purchase any sort of curiosities, So long as provisions etc are wanting & on the Spot to be sold; but in case of failure thereof, and the same being notified by the officers superintending the Trade, every person shall be at liberty to purchase what he pleaseth, provided he complies with the 2$^{\underline{d}}$ Article—

4$^{th}$ Art. All detached parties either in boats or on Shore shall be allowed to Trade for provisions &c not only for their own consumption, but for the general Stock—

5$^{th}$. All provisions & other refreshments procured by any person whatever & not consumed on shore, shall be brought publickly on the Quarter Deck & afterwards distributed out in such a manner as circumstances shall make appear most equitable—

Wednesday 18$^{th}$. at Day Light the Launches of both ships, with the Resolutions's great Cutter went to try if they could recover the Anchor &c that were left behind on the 16th At Noon they returned with the Resolutions Best Bower Anchor—Our Coasting Anchor had been weighd but when almost up, the Buoy Rope broke—a Swell setting in at the same time obliged the Boats to return—the Boats went again the next morning but returned without success; So that we have lost our Coasting Anchor &

---

[1] When Samuel Wallis was at Tahiti in 1767, some of the *Dolphin's* men had removed iron nails from the ship's timbers to trade for the personal favours of the local women. On Cook's first voyage, a seaman had stolen nails from the ship's store for the same purpose.—Hugh Carrington (ed.), *The Discovery of Tahiti. A Journal of the Second Voyage of H.M.S. Dolphin ... written by her master, George Robertson* (London, 1948), pp. 207–9; Beaglehole, *Cook Journals*, I, pp. 76, 98; See also Lewis de Bougainville, *A Voyage Round the World*, trans. J. R. Forster (London, 1772), p. 226.

Cable, 2 Small Anchors & 3 Hawsers[1]—every day during our stay here, we sent our Sick people (such as were able to go) on shore for a Walk & brought them off in the Evening—they all mend very fast[2]—

The Inhabitants of Otaheite Ete some months ago, made war upon Oteheite Nua, then under the command of Tutahaw, who was taken prisoner with many of his followers in a battle, several being killed on both sides—The day after the battle the merciless Conquoror put Tutahaw & some more of the chief prisoners to death. The Chief Aree here, knowing Capt[n] Cook was a Tio (friend) of Tutahaw, on our coming retired to the Mountains— Tutahaw was succeeded by Otu, the present Aree of Otaheite Nua[3]—

Some French Ships have been at this Island lately—the Inhabitants told us one of their men had run away & was then on the Island—on our making an Enquiry they afterwards denied it—many of our people & the Resolution's said they saw him amongst a number of the Inhabitants drest in the fashion of the Country. one of the men spoke to him in broken french, "parly vou francee Mons[r] the suposed Frenchman made no answer, but on the question being repeated ran away laughing— I won't pretend to determine whether or not this was a Frenchman

[1] With her bower anchor recovered, the *Resolution* had lost only 'a few fathms of Cable and about 150 fathm of 3 Inch rope'. Despite the *Adventure's* losses, Cook was not unduly perturbed: 'When I consider ye Dangerous situation we were in I cannot but think my self happy in coming off so well.'— Beaglehole, *Cook Journals*, II, p. 202 n. 4.

[2] According to Cook, the recovery of the sick men was greatly aided by fresh fruit. On 24 August, a week after the ships' arrival, he stated that many of the men who 'were so weak when we put in as not to be able to get on deck without assistance were now so far recovered as to be able to Walk about of themselves'. By the time the ships left Tahiti on 1 September, the sick men were 'all pretty well recovered'.—Beaglehole, *Cook Journals*, II, pp. 205, 210.

[3] Burney, like other voyagers, interpreted Tahitian affairs in the light of European political experience. Tahiti's complex political history is discussed by R. W. Williamson, *The Social and Political Systems of Central Polynesia* (3 vols, Cambridge, 1924), Vol. I, pp. 196–8. Tuteha, a prominent chief *(arii)* in Tahiti-nui at the time of Cook's first voyage, had been killed in an inter-district battle. Tu, who subsequently unified Tahiti as Pomare I, had emerged as the dominant political figure. However, like most historians of Tahiti, Williamson places too much reliance on Henry Adams, *Memoirs of Arii Taimai* (Paris, 1901). The problems involved in reconstructing the pre-Christian political history of Tahiti are discussed by Niel Gunson, 'A Note on the Difficulties of Ethnohistorical Writing, with Special Reference to Tahiti', *Journal of the Polynesian Society*, 72 (1963), pp. 415–19.

but I am very much inclined to think our people were mistaken—
however M.ʳ Foster wrote a Letter in French which he gave to
one of the Natives, but we never heard the fate of it[1]—
We cut 2 Scuttles in the Ships Sides, while we staid here, to give
more Air betwixt decks—

Tuesday 24th in the morning we hove our Anchors up & saild
from this place, the Commodore leaving his Cutter behind to
try if they could procure any more Hogs—the next day (25.ᵗʰ)
the Cutter returned about Noon with 10 which were divided
between the 2 Ships—at 7 this Evening we Anchord in Matavia
Bay[2] in 10 fathoms & Moord with our Small Bower & Stream
Anchors Bearings. Point Venus N. 1/4 E. End of the Reef N.W.
Westernmost part of the Island S.W. b W. & York Island[3] (Body
of it) W.S.W. ½ W.

the 26ᵗʰ We got the Tents of both Ships—with the Astronomers
Tents, Instruments &c on shore & the Resolution's Marines
were sent for a Guard—in the Afternoon all our Sick were sent
to the Tents—so that we made a very formidable appearance on
shore—there being in all 5 tents—The Marine officer having one.

We found it as difficult to get Hogs here as at Otaheite Ete—
we however got plenty of Roots Vegetables &c & our people all
recovered—One of the Resolutions Marines died here of the
Dropsy & was carried at a distance out at Sea & Buried—

September 1ˢᵗ having compleated our Water & overhauld the
Rigging, &c &c We Struck our Tents, got every thing on board
& saild in the Evening—

2.ᵈ In the Afternoon Saw the Society Isles—we lay too all Night
& the Next day stood in for Huaheine[4]—turning into the Harbour,

---

[1] The only European ship which had recently visited Tahiti was the Spanish
frigate *Aguila* (see p. 62 n. 4). Georg Forster, a naturalist on board the *Resolution*,
correctly refers to a Spanish, not a French, ship and states that the natives
had informed him the man was now dead.—Beaglehole, *Cook Journals*, II,
pp. 204–5 n. 4; Johann Georg Adam Forster, *A Voyage Round the World, in His
Britannic Majesty's Sloop, Resolution, Commanded by Capt. James Cook, During the
Years 1772, 3, 4 and 5* (2 vols, London, 1777), Vol. I, p. 308.
[2] Matavai Bay.
[3] Moorea.
[4] Huahine.

the passage being narrow & we coming too soon after the Resolution, we missed* Stays & fell on the Northern Reef where we lay 2 hours before we got off, without receiving any damage except breaking our Stream Anchor—in the Afternoon we got in & anchord in 17 fms—Extremes of Huaheine Island bearing North & South—Entrance of the Harbour between the Reefs from W.N.W. to W.S.W.

At this Small Island we (both Ships together) did not get less than 400 Hogs, large & small, from 80 pounds to Roasters—here one of the Inhabitants came on board & asked to go to England—Captain Cook likewise got an Indian, who was afterward seduced away at Ulietea[1] by a Girl—but he got another there who is a Relation of the famous Opoone[2]—

7th. Left this Island & next day got into Ohamaneno[3] Harbour in *Ulietea*—& Moord—Bearings Extremes of Ulietea in Sight N.N.E. & S. 3/4 E.t Entrance of the Harbour from N.W. b W. ½ W. to S.W. B W.½ W. *Peak of Bolabola*[4] N.W.½ N. depth 30 fthms both here & at Huaheine there is good Anchorage & shoaler water farther in—

14th. the *Resolution*'s Launch & our Cutter were sent over to the Island of Otahaw[5] to get fruit, it not being in such plenty here however we got as many Hogs as we knew what to do with—

16th this Afternoon the Boats returned well loaded—the Next Morning we weighd our Anchors & drifted out of the Harbour At Noon we took our Departure from the Land—bearings, Extremes of Ulietea E.N.E. & E. B S.—dist 5 or 6 Leagues. the body of the Otaha Id. N.Et. High peak of Bolabola N.1/4 E.— the Chart I have made of these Islands is copied from Captn Cook's only adapted to a Smaller Scale, that one side of the book might contain them. NB It was my intention to have made a neater one.[6]

[1] Raiatea.
[2] Puni. See pp. 72-3, p. 73 n. 1.
[3] Haamanino Harbour.
[4] Bora-Bora.
[5] Tahaa.
[6] There is no chart of the Society Islands in Burney's manuscript.
* *when in attempting to put a Ship about, She comes almost head to wind, but for want of having sufficient way through the water or from any other cause She refuses to be governd by the helm & turns back again, this is called missing Stays*

These Islands have been described in so satisfactory a manner, that there is no room left for me to hold forth without making frequent repetitions of what has before been said—never the less I will venture a word or two & attempt to draw their characters according to my own opinions[1]—

I must confess I was a little disappointed on my first coming here as I expected to find People nearly as white as Europeans. Some of the better sort are tolerably white, more so than a Spaniard or Portugueze, but the generality are of a dark olive Colour. the men are something larger than the common run in England—

The Similitude of Customs & Language scarce admits any doubt of these Islanders being sprung from the same stock as the Zealanders though from the difference of climate & country they are as opposite in their characters as the enervated, luxurious Italians & the rude unpolished Northern Nations of Europe—the Heavoh & Tattow are common to both though practised in different manners—the Islanders have I think, the Advantage of the Zealanders, in their persons, they are likewise very cleanly, washing both before & after every meal, & take a great deal of Pride in their Dress—any thing showy or Ornamental is much more esteemed here than at Zealand—especially by the girls who have almost as much Vanity as the Women of Europe—Hospitality & a love of Society reigns through all these Islands; I never in any of my Rambles met with an unwelcome reception—In short they are a friendly humane people, superior to the Zealanders in many aspects—I mean the men as to the women, they must not be mentiond together unless by way of contrast—they are reckon'd smaller here than the English Women & not in proportion to the men, but take away our high heads & high heels, the difference of Size would not be perceptible—there are much handsomer women in England & many, more ordinary. I mean as to the face—but for fine turned Limbs & well made persons I think they cannot be excelled—I only speak from my own notions, which are not infallible, for I have not the least pretence to

---

[1] Burney's 'own opinions' appear to be based largely on the observations of earlier European voyagers such as Wallis, Cook and Banks. Another likely source of information was the *Adventure's* Captain, Tobias Furneaux, who had previously visited Tahiti as second lieutenant in Wallis's ship, the *Dolphin*. Burney offers some original material based on his conversations with Omai (see pp. 71-5, 79, 80).

set up for a Judge in this case—the Children are in general exceeding beautifull—as they grow up they lose it for want of that care which in Europe is taken to preserve Beauty, they are not in the least afraid "The Winds of the Heavens Should visit their faces too roughly"—were they brought up in the delicate manner European Women are, there would be a great many very fine women amongst these Islands—Colour, in my opinion, has very little to do with beauty provided it be a healthy one it is a handsome one whether fair, brown or black—I question if they have any Idea of Chastity being a virtue—you may see young Girls not more than 12 years old with bellies they can scarce carry—after Marriage they confine themselves to the Husband—if they are caught slipping the Husband commonly sends them home to their Relations, but the Gallant does not escape so well, his life often paying the forfeit of his incontinence. the Independent men, or Aree's are allowed to have 2 wives— If a women after 6 or 7 months cohabitation with her Husband does not prove with Child, their Union, if they please, may be dissolved & each party at liberty to choose another mate. the women always mess by themselves & are seldom allowed to eat flesh—if a girl becomes pregnant the man cannot be forced to marry her. When a man courts any girl for a wife, after having got her relations consent, he sleeps 3 nights at their house—if the bride is a Virgin he is allowed to take no liberties till the 3$^{\text{d}}$ Night, though he lyes with her each Night—the 3$^{\text{d}}$ Day he makes the Relations a present & the 4$^{\text{th}}$ takes the Bride home—they give no portions with the girls unless the Bride's father has no Male children or other Male Relations to bestow his property on. a case which must be very rare in these Islands—

Otu who is the present Aree dehi[1] of Otaheite Nua is a very Stout man & I should think, likely were it not for a suspicious & ill natured look that prejudices me against him—he is not married & seems resolved to continue Single—but he makes free with any woman that Strikes his fancy, married or Unmarried, none daring to refuse him—& I question if it is thought any dishonour to be cukolded by the Aree dehi—Otu is remarkable for his inconstancy, keeping no woman more than 2 or 3 days— while we lay at Matavia Bay Captain Cook sent one of his

---

[1] *arii rahi*: a high-ranking chief, usually of a political district.

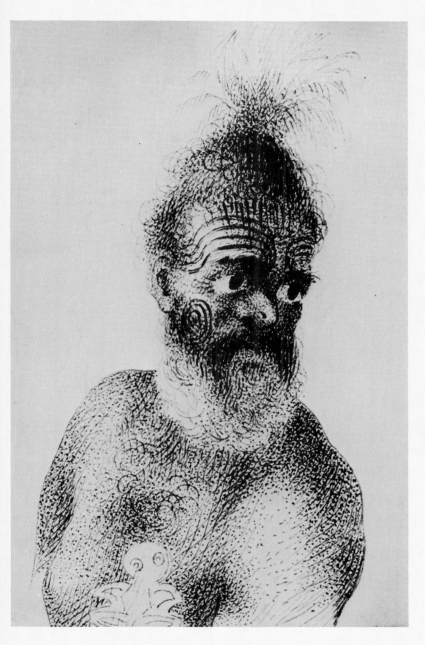

Plate 5. A South Sea Islander,
reproduced from the pen drawing, 10.2 x 8.2cm,
by William Hodges in the Petherick Collection,
National Library of Australia.

Plate 6. Omai, reproduced from the pencil drawing, 26.4 x 19.8cm, by Sir Joshua Reynolds in the Rex Nan Kivell Collection, National Library of Australia.

Lieutenants (M.ʳ Pickersgill) with a boat to a place calld Oparree[1]
—he there saw Obreea who was Queen of the Island when Capt.ⁿ
Wallace was here in the Dolphin[2]—Afterwards Tutahaw her
brother[3] was Aree but since his death Obreea has been neglected
& complains she has not the least interest with the present Aree—
M.ʳ P. asked her why she did not come to Matavai (the Bay we
lay in) & see her old friends—She answerd She had no presents
to bring & did not choose to come empty handed, it looked too
much like begging—She had been at the trouble of getting a
Number of Hogs & other things, but was not sufficed to take them
to the Ship. Captain Wallace had given Obreea a great many
things amongst which were 2 Geese—3 Guinea Hens—a Turkey
cock & Hen & a Cat—of these the Indian on board us, gave the
following account. 1 of the Geese died—the Guinea hens were
Stole from her & killed—the Turkey hen had 5 young ones but
the cat killd them all. the Cat who was with kitten miscarried,
was stole & carried away to another Island & the Turkey hen
is since dead—So unlucky has Obreea been with these presents[4]—

The Government here in one respect resembles that of the
Poles—there are but 2 classes of people, the Arees or Independent
Men & the Towtows or Servants—nor are the peasants of Poland
more subject or dependent on their Nobility than the Towtows on
their respective Arees or Masters[5]—

[1] Papara, a district in the south of Tahiti-nui.
[2] Purea had not been the 'Queen' of the whole island but the wife of Amo,
*arii rahi* of Papara. Purea's predominance has since been exaggerated by most
historians of Tahiti who have relied on Henry Adam's *Memoirs of Arii Taimai*,
written largely by a descendant of Purea. The role of Purea and her family
in Tahitian politics is discussed by Gunson, *Journal of the Polynesian Society*,
72, pp. 415–19, and Robert Langdon, 'A View on Ari'i Taimai's Memoirs',
*Journal of Pacific History*, 4 (1969), pp. 162–5.
[3] According to Williamson, *Social and Political Systems*, Vol. I, p. 191, Tuteha
was not Purea's brother but her 'brother's wife's brother'. Tuteha, *arii rahi*
of Atehuru, had dominated the western region of Tahiti.
[4] Apart from the animals, Wallis gave Purea an assortment of glassware
and tools as a parting gift. During his stay at Tahiti in June-July 1767, Wallis
had conducted a thriving trade with Purea, trading European goods chiefly
for hogs.—Wallis, *Dolphin Log*. PRO Adm. 55/35. Entries for 12–27 July 1767.
[5] Burney made similar errors to other voyagers in attempting to understand
the complex socio-political structure of the Society Islands. In over-simplified
terms, there were three basic classes: the *arii*—district (or sub-district) chiefs;
the *ra'atira*—landowners and also keepers of the lands of the *arii*; and the
*manahune*—landless commoners. The *teu-teu* were not the lowest class, as Cook
and Banks had also stated, but members of the *manahune* class who served the
*arii* as hereditary servants.—See Teuira Henry, *Ancient Tahiti*, Bernice P.
Bishop Museum Bulletin 48 (Honolulu, 1928), pp. 229–46.

N.B. Every independent man is called an Aree—

The Custom of getting a Tio[1], or particular friend is the most comfortable way of proceeding, but the most expensive—Your Tio exchanges Names with you—you are always welcome at his house & whatever you want he'll procure you; this Custom is mentioned, I think, by Magellan or some Spaniard who stopd at one of the Islands hereabouts[2]—Some of these Tio's are very interested & when they make any present expect a return that in the common way of trading would purchase treble the worth of theirs—They called me Teparny which unfortunately happening to be the name M<sup>r</sup> Banks went by,[3] induced several to offer me presents & desire to change Names—but my first Tio was so continually begging & hard to satisfy that I commonly declined their civility with as good a grace as I could.—not providing myself with a sufficient Stock of Trade when I left England made me unable to afford it. I parted with every thing that I could any ways contrive to Spare & with difficulty refrain from selling my Cloaths—had we staid much longer at these Islands, few of the younkers in either ship would have had a Shirt left—

The Indian who came on board us is named Omy,[4] though we commonly call him Jack. he is a fellow of quick parts—very intelligent, has a good memory & takes great notice of every thing he sees. he is possessed of many good qualities—is Strong, active, healthy & as likely to weather the hardships of a long Voyage as any of us—he was at Otaheite at the time of their attacking the Dolphin & got wounded in the action—from this man I gather almost all my intelligence concerning these Islands Omy is the Second Son of an Independent man & was one of the under priests or assistants to the high priest of Huaheine—he has been a great traveller, having been at most of the Islands within their knowledge[5]—we got him at different times to make

---

[1] *taio*.

[2] Magellan had not called at any of the islands in the area. Burney was possibly thinking of Pedro Fernandez de Quiros, who had established friendly relations with the natives of Hao in the Tuamotu Archipelago in February 1606.—Clements Markham (ed.), *The Voyages of Pedro Fernandez de Quiros, 1595 to 1606* (London, 1944), pp. 334–40.

[3] In his journal, Banks mentions the practice of obtaining a *taio* but gives no names.—Beaglehole, *Endeavour Journal*, I, pp. 253, 255.

[4] Omai (Omy, Omiah).

[5] Unlike the unfortunate Tobia of Cook's first voyage (see p. 49 n. 3), Omai survived the voyage to England where he spent two years before returning to the Society Islands on Cook's third voyage.

2 Draughts of them to see how they agreed—he put down nearly the same number in each & gave the same names—but in respect of situation they would not bear comparison—he says none of these Islands are equal to Otaheite or larger than Ulietea—

Some of these Islands are inhabited by People who speak a different Language from the Otaheiteans—of these Omy has seen five which he describes to be low Islands laying 7 or 8 days Sail to the Eastward—their Names are Mativa, Orieduar, Moduoho, Oteouyou & Mattaer—the 4 first are in sight of one another, the last 3 or 4 Days Sail to the Southward[1]—the Men are tattowd with a streak from the Corners of the Mouth to their Ears. the Women under the Neck from Ear to Ear—The Society Islanders came but lately to the knowledge of these Islands, by the following accident. 2 Canoes from Mativa were overtaken by a gale of Wind & drove to the N.W.—they had been near a month at Sea when they saw Otaheite & Huaheine & made towards the latter, having had nothing to eat for the last 3 or 4 days—the Aree of Huaheine entertained them in a friendly manner, but took away both their Canoes & gave them one of his own to return in. A Man & Woman of Mativa Staid behind & now live at Huaheine. Omy mentions an Island called Oevah where are men of a gigantic Size & who are Cannibals— he never saw any of those people, nor knows how far or which way they lay[2]—of the Islands where the Otaheite language is spoken he mentions no more than what has already been seen by Captⁿ Wallace & Captⁿ Cook & all these he has visited himself.

Omy amongst other adventures he relates of himself, was once taken by the Bolabola men in an Engagement between 2 large Canoes—Tereroa—then Aree of Huaheine, Elder brother of

[1] These islands, stretching south-east from Mataiva, were situated in the north-west extremity of the Tuamotu Archipelago. As Omai said later, they were north-east rather than east of the Society Islands (see p. 81, p. 81 n. 1). When the *Resolution* visited the adjacent King George's Islands in April 1774, a native on board from Raiatea in the Society Islands could not understand the local language.—Beaglehole, *Cook Journals*, II, p. 377 n. 3.

[2] This was probably Uvea, situated approximately two thousand miles west of Tahiti. It was also known as Wallis Island after a visit by Samuel Wallis in August 1767. Neither Wallis nor George Robertson, the *Dolphin's* major chronicler, had commented that the natives were either particularly large or were cannibals. Robertson stated only that they were 'all strong well made men'.—Carrington, *The Discovery of Tahiti*, p. 255; Wallis, *Log*, PRO Adm. 55/35, entry for 17 August 1767.

Oree[1] the present Aree was killed in the battle & the prisoners carried to Bolabola—Omy & 6 more were saved by the Intercession of a Ulietea woman who lived there & was an old Tio of one of them—this clemency occasioned great disputes, for these Islanders Seldom show any favour to their prisoners—The Huaheine men not liking their precarious situation resolved to attempt their escape—on the 2$^d$ Night as soon as all was quiet they stole out & found a Canoe which they carried in their Arms down to the Water—they afterwards took the paddles from under a Bolabola man's head, one softly lifting his head up while another drew out the paddles—as they had a long way to go against the wind and no place where they darest stop—they could not venture without a stock of provisions, which they procured with equal dexterity—one of them got a Young Hog & to prevent his making a noise, held him hard by the snout till he came to the water side, then plunged him in and kept him under till he was drownd—they had hardly got clear when they met a large Bolabola Canoe who askd them several questions—Omy who had been at Bolabola before answerd, imitating the Voice and manner of the Bolabola men—it being dark they passed on without suspicion & next night got to Huaheine—in the Battle Omy lost 4 Relations—the Huaheine men sometime ago were in a manner subjected to Opune—a great many Bolabola men living on their Island—Tereroa had soon reason to be tired of their company—he took an opportunity when Opune was absent, to send Canoes privately to Ohaha for a Number of Men to assist him—these landed unknown to the Bolabola men who were attackd the Same Night—asleep & unprepared—& most of them killed—Opune soon after killed Tereroa in the Engagement above mentioned—since this he has attempted to regain his footing in Huaheine but by the bravery & conduct of Oree, has been unable to effect it. Otaha however could not withstand him—both that & Ulietea are subject to him.

Opune has but one child (a Girl) living; he has 2 Wives & 3 Concubines—Tereroa's Sister was formerly one of his wives—She has been dead some time his Daughter if She survives him will inherit his Dominions—for he is not likely to have any more Children, being now a very old man—but is Still greatly loved by his own Subjects & feared by the other Islands—

[1] Ori.

Opune, in spite of old age & Blindness, (his Eyes being very bad) nevertheless retains all the Chearfullness & Merriment of a Young Man, nor are his people ever happier than when in his Company—he is a great encourager of their Games & Revels (their Heavah of which I shall Speak presently) & has invented many new ones himself—I have given this Character of him from what Omy says, who stiles him a fighting man & a man of Laughter.—I never saw him[1]—

Of these people's Character, I have as yet shewn you only the fair Side—My partiality towards them shall not induce me to Stop here—As I set down nought in Malice, so will I nothing extenuate.

In their dealings with us they are great thieves, our Goods being of such Value to them, that very few can withstand the temptation of a fair opportunity—nevertheless I have slept all Night in their houses 3 miles up the Country, without any attempt being made on me—theft amongst themselves is punished with Death—

They have some very barbarous customs, the worst of which is, when a man has as many children as he is able to maintain, all that come after are smothered: women will sometimes bargain with her husband on her first marrying him, for the Number of Children that shall be kept. they never keep any Children that are any ways deformed—every fifth Child if suffered to live is Seldom allowed to rank higher than a Towtow—yet notwithstanding all this, these Islands are exceeding populous— even the Smallest being full of inhabitants & perhaps were it not for the Custom just mentioned, these would be more than the Islands could well maintain—

Every Island has a high priest, some two, with inferior priests— of this latter Class was Omy—the Being whom they worship they call Mo-wee[2] & sometime offer human sacrifices to him—[3]this is

---

[1] On his first voyage in 1769, Cook had met Puni who was 'then very old'.— Beaglehole, *Cook Journals*, I, p. 150; II, p. 233.

[2] *Maui* was a prominent figure in Polynesian mythology but not, as Burney suggests, the only 'being' worshipped. He was, in fact, not so much a god as a culture hero. Burney's portrayal of the religious beliefs and ceremonies of the Society Islanders is extremely oversimplified.— See E. S. Craighill Handy, *Polynesian Religion*, Bernice P. Bishop Museum Bulletin 34 (Honolulu, 1927).

[3] Four years later, in September 1777, Cook witnessed 'this extraordinary and barbarous custom' at a ceremony near Matavai Bay in Tahiti.—Beaglehole, *Cook Journals*, III, pp. 198–205.

not done at any particular sett times but when Mo-wee requires it—he appears to none but the high priests, who frequently pretend to see him flying—this gives the high priest great power & if he is a man of a vindictive temper, whoever offends him must feel it—Mo-wee always names the person & as soon as his desires are known to the high priest he sends his attendants to dispatch the destined victim who knows nothing of his fate till the minute of his death—having killed him, he is carried to the high Priest, who takes out his Eyes, which Mo-wee eats, & the body is buried—

Before they venture on any extraordinary Expedition, Mo-wee is consulted: if the priest brings bad News it is either laid aside or deferred till better success is promised. Temperance or Chastity is not in the least essential to the high priest's Character, he being at liberty to take any woman he chooses to honour so far, married or unmarried, for as long as he pleases. The great power of the high priest would be very inconvenient for the Chief Aree were it not that they most commonly exercise this office themselves.— The Kingsfisher is one of their inferior deities—& the high priest understands what they say—

The people at particular times are all assembled together. The high priest & under priest Stand in the middle the people sitting down in a ring round them—Silence is then commanded & the high priest holding a small bunch of feathers in his hand, Speechifies—he then gives the feathers to one of the under priests who makes an Oration in his turn—thus they speak alternately, the feathers being held by the Speaker—Omy repeats Speeches or rather songs which Oree & himself deliver to the people— but what is very extraordinary, is, their preaching is not in the common language, but in a language, or Cant, invented purposely for this occasion—few or none of the Audience understand what the priest says—& I question whether he understands himself— when I ask Omy the meaning of any particular word or part of these speeches, he tells me it is perrow tou-a-*priest talk* this Lingo consists in a number of Short Sentences—of which the following is a Specimen—

Oete vow a taer
O'-ette a no oette awry
Outu bo tu tou noua
mahorotony arawutta popy c derro
eo o ete bo
owy te bu e nea—&c &c—

Opune, who is Chief priest of the Islands under him, is as much Superior in this capacity as in any other. The high priests of the other Islands sometimes pretend to see their Mowee, but Opune takes the Mowee of Bolabola in his Arms & shows him in publick— their Mowee is a fish with a man's head, one Arm & one fin— this farce is acted at one of the little Islands Tubai, whither Opune always goes when he wants to consult him—After preaching he goes down to the Water Side & prays Mowee to come & resolve their doubts—the Obedient God appears & is questioned—if he Nods it signifies Approbation. on receiving a favourable answer the priest Steps in the Water & holds Mowee in his Arms for the Admiring Crowd to gaze at—10 priests are allotted to attend this Mowee—they live by turn on the Island & no one else is sufferd to go there except on publick days—Omy has been present when this *gentleman* has been consulted & has no notion of any deception or slight being practised. *he* professes to believe every thing that is given out by the high priest—perhaps he was not far enough advanced to be let into their Secrets—or else out of regard to his profession he pretends a belief which he has not—

during our stay at Huaheine, Mr Speerman (a gentleman on board the Resolution who assisted M<sup>r</sup> Foster in Botanical affairs) venturing too far up the Country by himself, was sett upon by 4 or 5 men & stript of every thing but one Shoe—one of them who had his hanger made a cut at him, but luckily it was with the back part of the weapon—they then left him & he was obliged to wander some time naked in the middle of the day before he could see any body, for the Robbery was committed at a distance from any habitation—the first house he came to the people flockd about him & when they understood he had been robbed, did every thing in their power to relieve him—he wrapt a piece of their Cloth round him & in that condition came down to the Water Side where the 2 Captains were—they complaind to Oree who immediately sent in quest of the Robbers & soon after as the Capt<sup>ns</sup> were getting in their boat to go on board, the Hanger

& part of the Cloaths were brought back—Capt$^n$ Cook not seeming content with this, Oree promised a search should be made for the Offenders who had hid themselves in the Mountains, & that they Should be punished—& that Capt$^n$ Cook might have no doubt of his Sincerity insisted on going on board to dine with Him—the Natives begd. & prayd went on their knees & did all they could to dissuade him but he told them he had no reason to be afraid, that he was no Theif & Capt$^n$ Cook was his friend—in the Evening the Captains went ashore with him but saw nothing of the Thieves—the next morning we saild for Ulietea—we had got about a mile without Huaheine Harbour when we saw a Canoe coming after us. Capt$^n$ Cook brought too to see what they wanted, & received a message from Oree, signifying the Teto's (Thieves) were taken, and desiring him to come ashore and see them punishd—this was declined it not being of consequence enough to detain the Ships—but it shews the honesty of Oree—he was Capt$^n$ Cooks Tio last Voyage—& went by his name while we staid there[1]

At Ulietea I saw one of their Heava's or dances. I shall only say of their dancing that in 5 minutes time they commonly go through all their manoeuvres—the rest is a continual repetition—but what afforded me much more entertainment, was at every interval between their dancing, small dramatic pieces were acted by way of interludes to intertain the Spectators while the dancers took breath. These were performd by men. they have a great deal of good action. one in particular whom we nicknamed Garrick expressed the passions so lively in his looks, Voice & actions that we easily dived into his meaning & understood the plots of most of their pieces—Every now and then the Spectators would break into immoderate fits of laughter at some jest which was lost to us from our little knowledge of their language—

---

[1] Anders Sparrman was a young Swedish physician and assistant to naturalist J. R. Forster. Unlike Burney, who gives a picture of Sparrman left with only a shoe, Cook states that Sparrman was robbed of everything 'but his Trowsers'. Sparrman's own description of the incident suggests that he managed to retain both his trousers and a shoe. A further exaggeration on Burney's part is his statement that Sparrman had four or five attackers; both Sparrman and Cook say there were two.—Owen Rutter (ed.), *Anders Sparrman. A Voyage Round the World with Captain James Cook in H.M.S. Resolution*, trans. Huldine Beamish and Averil Mackenzie-Grieve (London, 1953), pp. 78–81; Beaglehole, *Cook Journals*, II, p. 218.

however we were able to comprehend the Story—

I will give you a small account of one

The Master of a family before Night puts every thing in its proper place & sees all in order—after which the whole family go to sleep presently in comes the Thief who conveys every thing he lays hold of to his Companions who wait without—after playing many dextrous tricks one of the family wakes & alarms the rest—they all get up & grope about the Thief (you are to supose it quite dark) & one of them gets hold of his Cloaths which the Thief immediately slips off, puts over a post & makes his escape—the other all this time holds fast & calls for a light, thinking he had caught the Rogue—the light comes & he is undeceivd—& finds every thing moveable carried off—The Master falls in a passion, beats his Servants for their Carelessness they promise to behave better & the piece concludes—

This, you'll say, is not poetical justice. unless they account Negligence a greater crime than dishonesty.

One Evening while we lay here (at Ulietea) Omy staid on shore—in the middle of the Night he came off naked, leaving his Jacket & Trowsers behind him nor would he go ashore again during our Stay—it seems a report had Spread amongst the Islanders that Omy was going to *Britannia* to get poopooe's (guns) of the Aree, to kill the bolabola men—probably he might himself be the Author of this report but however that be, the Bolabola men Who lived at Ulietea were contriving to prevent, or rather to finish his Travels—he had notice of this given him by an acquaintance who awoke him out of his sleep & advised him to get off as fast as he could—accordingly without regarding his Cloaths, he took to the water & Swam to a fishing Canoe who put him aboard.

These Islanders when they are much offended at any thing, will stop all manner of communication, & till the Aree is pacified not a Canoe will come near the Ship—if a boat goes ashore, they will keep at a distance & hardly Speak to us. Sending us to Coventry—this happend to us once at Otaheite ete & once here— the first was on account of firing at a Canoe that had stole something & bringing her on board—but next day all was made up & every thing went on as before—the 2ᵈ was a more serious affair & lasted 2 or 3 days during which time we had no intercourse with the Natives—nor could we understand them well enough to know the Cause—they mentiond something of a woman being

wounded, but how or which way we could not cleverly make out[1]—
'tis likely they had too much reason for their Complaints Some
of our young folks behaving in a very foolish, arrogant manner
drawing their Swords to fright them & pretending to be in a passion
at trifles—this probably may be the occasion of others being ill
used, as M.ʳ Speerman was at Huaheine—

it is not safe at any of the Islands, for a single person to wander
too far from any houses, Speerman was not the only instance of
people suffering by it—however in the houses, or amongst a
Multitude you are safe from Robbers but not from Pickpockets,
of which there are always enough on the watch to take advantage
of your Negligence—

The Music at these Islands is less worth Notice than at Zealand,
so I shall say nothing more on that score—

Mem.ᵈᵘᵐˢ Rock off Charlotte Sound not laid down in the Chart
Mr Gilbert sent out by Capt.ⁿ Cook to Survey it[2]—

Sunday April 25ᵗʰ The first Time in Charlotte Sound—The Tent
ashore at the South part of the Motuara—this day the Ship
shifted her Birth from off the Motuara into Ship Cove—taking
bearings & getting Shells in the Jolly Boat with M.ʳ Wilby one of
the Midshipmen & M.ʳ Young the Surgeons 2ᵈ Mate, Chased by
the New Zealanders and narrowly excaped being taken (2 Canoes)
when we got in sight of the Ship they fired a 4 pounder the Shot
fell right between us—on which the Canoes stopt—got ashore to
the Tent and put ourselves on our guard then let the Indians
come ashore—staid with us till Sunsett & we parted very good
friends—these Indians came from the Northward[3]

*In Charlotte Sound New Zealand 1st Time*

[1] According to Third Lieutenant Richard Pickersgill, the Raiateans had
'fled to the Mountains' after two young seamen, whom they had taken captive,
threatened that Cook would go ashore and kill them all when he found out
about their behaviour.—R. Pickersgill, *Journal* (National Maritime Museum,
Greenwich, 57/038). Extract printed in Beaglehole, *Cook Journals*, II, pp.767-75.

[2] This event had taken place over three months earlier on 24 May 1773,
before the ships left New Zealand. The man concerned was Joseph Gilbert,
Master of the *Resolution*.—Beaglehole, *Cook Journals*, II, p. 167.

[3] This was another incident which had occurred while the *Adventure* was
at Queen Charlotte Sound (see p. 51).

*Memorandums*                                                    Society Islands

Omy says the Bolabola men destroy none of their Children and they are the only people, amongst these Islands, who do not. The consequence of which is, they are more numerous than the rest, and great numbers of them have found means to settle themselves on every one of the other Islands—When Opune wants to collect his forces on any extraordinary occasion he sends private notice to the Bolabola men & they immediately obey the summons and transport themselves to the place of Rendezvous—

I shall mention one more instance of Opune's superiority— The Otaheiteans made Shift to purchase a large Anchor out of the ground that was left behind by Mons.<sup>r</sup> Bougainville they broke off one of the Arms and were foolish enough to carry the remainder about to the other Islands to be gazed at and admired. Opune saw & fell in love with it & they, *not out of fear* (so Omy says) but merely to oblige a man they wishd to the devil, made him a present of it

Bolabola men differently tattow<sup>d</sup> from the other Islanders the fighting men on their arms and breast—

On our Arrival at the Islands Opune retired to Maurua[1] and sent over for intelligence concerning Tobia, being afraid of his return & that the Ships w<sup>d</sup> take his part[2]—

Opune certainly must have been a sensible, fine fellow & it would be a pity to assist any one against him or his Country men the Bolabola men who are (in my opinion) superior *to the other Islanders—*

*Huaheine War Canoe*

Of the War Canoe at Huaheine. Mem<sup>d</sup> to get a plan of it—two large Canoes joined together by cross pieces at Small distances on each of which set a Row of Paddlers 5 in a Row. being 1 in the middle between the 2 Canoes & 2 on each side. without on the Crosspieces or Seats are fastned Small pieces of Bamboo which run parallel to the Canoes & serves to divide the Paddlers & makes their situation less precarious—a platform elevated

---

[1] Now Maupiti.
[2] Tobia had been an *arii* and priest of Raiatea before the island was subordinated to Puni of Bora-Bora.

about 7 feet above the Canoe Supported by Pillars badly carved—here the Slingers Archers & Spearmen stand—Mem<sup>dm</sup>. Enquire the Number of seats & paddles—

Their Astronomy. (know the planets from the fixed stars & call them by a different name) constellations—The 2 Small Stars close together in the Scorpion's tail they call the twins & 2 brighter ones that are near them are the father and mother—Story of them—

Mattibarie, a fisherman, had 2 Children (twins) a boy and a girl. by bad weather and worse luck he had lived several days on nothing but bread fruit—at last luck changd and one night, after the children had been sent to rest, he brought home a great quantity of fish—he and his wife immediately drest some & made a very hearty meal the wife desired the children might be called to partake, but the greedy fisherman would by no means consent. The Children happend to be awake all the time, but were afraid to speak and lay crying at their Fathers unkindness. Mowee took pity on them & sent down a Rope by which he hauld them up & placed them in the firmament. next morning the children were missing & the Mother in despair was going to kill herself, when Mowee took her up & placed her by her Children —The fisherman repented of his unkindness & at length Mowee through the intreaties of his wife and Children was prevaild on to forgive him—accordingly the hauling line was sent down & he was hoisted up as high as the rest of His family—All this, Omy says, happend just before his (Omy's) Grandfather was born there is a House at Huaheine called Mattibarie now & which he says stands on the same spot that Mattibaries house formerly stood—

Omy Says the memory and understanding are Lodged in the Belly. the head is only an instrument—the head sees and speaks but the Belly dictates—

Omy keeping account of the number of Days with Chips—terribly frightend the 2<sup>d</sup> Day after leaving the Society Islands—it being Sunday the people were calld to prayers—he seeing every body getting together, suspected it was to consult whether or not we should kill him—we were some time before we could learn the cause of his uneasiness & then it was with difficulty we were able to quiet his apprehensions—

Omy after our arrival at the Cape of good hope giving a quite different account of the Mativa Islands, making them all one Land much Larger than Otaheite & of which the Otaheite people don't know the End—he makes it to the N.E. & N$\underline{o}$.1 believe Omy is not always to be credited & that he is a Small matter addicted to romancing—

1773 Saturday September 18$^{th}$. Left the Society Islands in company with the Resolution—

September 23$^{d}$. passd by (to the Northw$^{d}$. of them) 2 Small low Islands of a very pleasant & fruitful appearance. not near enough to assertain whether or not they were inhabited[2]. Lat. 19..15 S$^{o}$. Long$^{d}$. 201..30 E$^{t}$. at Greenwich. Var 7° E$^{t}$

1773 October 1$^{st}$ in the Afternoon saw the Island of Middleburg bearing W.b S. 8 or 9 Leag$^{s}$ Stood off & on all Night & at day Light bore away for the South End, off which at about a League distant is a small pleasant Island[3]—we went within this & ran alongshore, from the South point, N.W. by the Compass 6 or 7 miles and rounded the West End whence the Shore runs nearly N.b E. by compass, about the same distance to the North End between, these 2 points we Anchord in 22 fath$^{ms}$ about 300 yards from the Shore extreems of the Land bearing N.N.E. & S. b E. from here we saw the Island of Amsterdam[4] bearing by compass from W. $\frac{1}{2}$ N. to N.N.W. $\frac{1}{2}$ W. dist$^{t}$ 5 Leagues

Anchorage, we anchord in an open Road to Leeward of the Island. bottom hard sand 22 fms—a strait shore—were obliged to run close in before we got ground—The Sun being to the Southward of the Line the Trade Wind is regular and the evenness of the Land prevents the true Course of the Wind from being interruped, that there is but little danger of flurries or Eddy Winds—
Lat$^{d}$ of Middleburg 21..17 S$^{o}$. Long$^{d}$ of West End 185..40E$^{t}$.
       to 21..29         Var$^{tn}$     10..30E$^{t}$
Extent from East to West 8 or 9 miles—

[1] Mataiva, a tiny island in the north Tuamotus, was one of a group of five islands which Omai had earlier stated were east of the Society Islands. See p. 71 n. 1
[2] Manuae and Aoutu in the lower Cook Islands.
[3] Kalau.
[4] In January 1643, Tasman had named Tongatapu and Eua, the two major islands in the southern Tongan group, Amsterdam and Middelburch (Middleburg) respectively.—Sharp, *Voyages of Tasman*, p. 153.

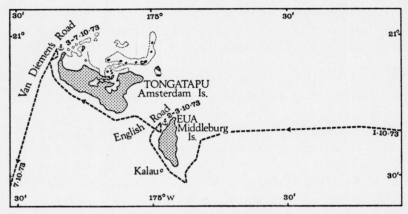

Fig. 5. Southern Tonga.

Middleburg calld Ow-hy by the Natives—

Appearance—the Land is quite level—may be seen in a clear day 8 Leagues from the Deck—its appearance on coming closer is as beautifull as can be imagined—equal to any Landscape I ever saw—

Natives friendly. got but little fruit or other refreshments here. their coming off to us without expressing the least Surprise or fear makes me imagine they have been visited lately by some Ship[1]—

October 3ᵈ early in the morning left this Island, having lain here but 21 Hours—and Saild for the Island of Amsterdam—

1773 October 3ᵈ at 11 am were abrest the S.E. point of Amsterdam which lies W.½ N. per Compass 5 leagˢ from where we lay at Anchor at Middleburg. from the S.E. point of Amsterdam the Shore runs per Compass W.½ N. & W. by N. 4 miles W.N.W. 7 miles & N.W.b N. about 3 miles to the West point of the Island whence the Land runs N.E.b N. a good League and turns short off to the Eastward. at ½ past 5 pm we Anchord between the North & West points of the Island about a quarter of a mile off shore in 27 fms fine sand. bad holding ground the N⁰ & West points of the Island bearing N.E. 1/4 E. & S.b W.½ W. A Shoal in the offing

---

[1] Burney was wrong. No European ship had visited either Eua or Tongatapu since Tasman in 1643. Samuel Wallis had called at Niuatoputapu, slightly north of the Tongan group, in 1767.—Carrington, *The Discovery of Tahiti*, pp. 249–53.

(dry at half Ebb) from N.W.b W. to W.N.W. $\frac{1}{2}$ W. distant 2 or 3 miles from the Island—round the North point of the Island are several small Islands & shoals— Lat$^{de}$ of

Amsterdam to $\begin{array}{l} 21 . . 02 \\ 21 . . 17 \end{array}$ S$^o_{\cdot}$ $\begin{cases} \text{Long}^d \text{ of W}^t_{\cdot} \text{ End } 0^\circ . . 30' \text{ from} (185 : 10 \text{E}^t_{\cdot}) \\ \text{the west End of Middleburgh} \end{cases}$

Extent of the Is$^d$ from E$^t_{\cdot}$ to West about 4 Leag$^s_{\cdot}$ Var$^{tn}$ 10..11 E$^t_{\cdot}$

The Resolution lost her Stream Anchor here—though our Cable was very little rubbd either here or at Middleburg

Tide rises 4 feet perpendicular, being tried when the Moon

H M

was 5 Days & 5 Hours past full. High water 7..51 After the Moon passed the Meridian—

No Watering place here for Shipping that we could discover Amsterdam Calld Tong-i by the Natives

lower Land & of greater extent than Middleburg—Natives, inferior in persons to the Society Islanders Not so cleanly, painting and greasing themselves—not so bad as described by Tasman[1]—

More industry, more ingenuity & more neatness in their work than the other Islanders

Language different. some words alike. g & R in their Alphabet which the Society Islanders cannot pronounce

tattowd here—

little fingers lopt off—people friendly & well desposed but great Thieves, on which account we had some quarrels with them—

The Resolutions Boat lay ashore with a grappling out & they had the Impudence and dexterity to cut the Rope and carry the graplin away under water—at least to remove it so far from where it was let go that we could not find it again[2]

October 5$^{\text{th}}_{\cdot}$ Tuesday. this morning the Inhabitants refused to let the Boat Land—on which Capt$^n$ Cook sent a party of marines on shore to guard the landing Place—all quiet after this—

---

[1] In January 1643, Tasman had described the natives of Nomuka (which he named Rotterdam), an island in the northern Tongan group, as having 'the form of a man but inhuman Morals and customs'.—Sharp, *Voyages of Tasman*, p. 170.

[2] Cook reported more instances of daring thefts by the natives of Tongatapu. One man took some books from the Master's cabin and another stole a seaman's jacket from one of the boats. Tasman had experienced similar problems 130 years earlier when a native visiting his ship made off with 'the Skipper's pistol with a pair of slippers'.—Beaglehole, *Cook Journals*, II, pp. 255–6; Sharp, *Voyages of Tasman*, p. 154.

Hogs plenty here. we did not much want them having a great many of our old stock left—

Fruit & Vegetables in great plenty of which we laid in a large Cargo—

Not much fresh water either here or at Middleburgh—that we saw—in wells & not very good.

Arms. Clubs Spears—Bows & Arrows—grove in the back of the Bow in which is a string of strong grass. this besides strengthening it helps the Elasticity of the Wood & sends an Arrow with great force—

Music. flat 3$^d$. they sing in parts, keeping the Same time and varying the 4 notes without ever going beyond them. So many singers & so few notes you always hear the whole together. the difference of Words & Voices make some variety. the Singers (that I heard) all were women. one confined herself entirely to the Lower Note which acted as a Drone. they sing slow and ended with the minor Chord it put me in mind of the Church Singing among the Roman Catholics—instruments, Flutes (Nosy) and Reed Organs[1]—

Under better government than the Society Isles—their houses & their Land being mostly within Enclosures & good Roads between—

Their Canoes—(Mem$^d$. get a plan of their Sailing Canoes) at the Society I$^{ds}$ the planks Butt

here the planks are scarfd[2]

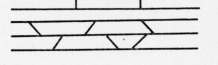

*Mem.* to get a plan of their Temples—

present brought down to the Water Side for Capt$^n$ Cook the Night before we saild—the Chief of the Island did not come—

---

[1] Burney gave a copy of this tune to Georg Forster, who thought Burney was 'a very ingenious gentleman'. According to Cook, the Tongans' songs were 'musical and harmonious, noways harsh or disagreeable'.—Forster, *Voyage Round the World*, I, p. 429; Beaglehole, *Cook Journals*, II, p. 246.

[2] The construction of Tongan canoes is described in detail by Beaglehole, *Cook Journals*, II, pp. 263–5. Two of Hodges' drawings of the canoes are reproduced in *ibid.*, figs 47, 48.

Plate 7. Tongatapu or Amsterdam Island. From the watercolour, 37.3 x 54.5cm, by William Hodges in the Rex Nan Kivell Collection, National Library of Australia.

Plate 8.   A man of New Zealand.
From the crayon drawing, 54.2 x 37.3cm,
by William Hodges in the National Library of Australia,
on permanent loan from the British Admiralty.

Thursday October 7th Saild this Forenoon. on the whole I like the Society Islands much better than these—on account of the People who are more friendly and sociable[1]—

We now made the best of our way for New Zealand in company with the Resolution Captn Cook—

1773 October 8th this afternoon saw the Isd of Pülstreet[2]—we did not come nearer than 7 Leagues. it is a small high Island. Latde 22..20 So Longde 0°..45' Wt from the west End of Amsterdam. (184..25 Et)—

October 21st we made the Table Cape on the East Side of North Zealand. in the Night we crossd Hawk's Bay[3] & ran to the S.W. alongshore being bound to Charlotte Sound—

Friday 22d this Forenoon passd Black Head—Some canoes came off to the Resolution for whom he lay too about half an hour—at sunset the Resolution was almost Hull down ahead— had a very boisterous Night, and next morning could see nothing of the Resolution—however the next day (the 24th) we fell in with her & joind Company again— being then off Cape Pallisser at the Entrance of Cooks Straits which Seperates the 2 Islands of New Zealand—

from this time we had a great deal of Blowing Weather & almost continual foul winds (N.W.). parted from the Resolution the Night of the 26th but joind her again on the 28th the 29th at Night we lost Sight of her the 3d Time after this we never had the good fortune to meet her again when we parted were close under Cape Pallisser—

Our Ship in her best trim is not able to keep up, or carry Sail with the Resolution—at this time we fall bodily to Leeward being quite Light & so crank that we are obliged to Strike to every Squall—and so unmanageable that there is no getting her round either one way or another. on the Morning of the 5th of November being near Cape Pallisser the Wind Shifted Suddenly from the N.W. to the S.S.W. & blew very strong—we had 3

---

[1] Cook was more impressed. He was 'highly dilighted' with the natives' 'friendly behaver' and, despite their thieving activities, later named the island group the 'Friendly Isles, or Archipelago'.—Beaglehole, Cook Journals, II, pp. 248, 449 n. 3.
[2] Pylstaert or Ata.
[3] Hawke Bay.

Tryals & were full 3/4 of an hour before we could get her head off shore—had she faild the 3$^d$ Time we should have cut away our Mizen Mast—

the Night of the 5$^{th}$ had a tolerable good chance being to the S.E. of Cape Pallisser Wind at South—but it being doubtfull whether we should be able to weather the Land (the Wind increasing and Night coming on) the Capt$^n$ did not think it Safe to trust the Ship on a Lee Shore—the next morning the Wind blowing hard from the Southward and we being too far to the Eastward to be able to weather Cape Pallisser we Bore away for Tolaga Bay (Nov$^{br}$ 6$^{th}$ at ½ past 8 am)[1]

from our being so often baffled in trying to get round Cape Pallisser our seamen new Christend it, by the Significant Name of Cape Turn and be damnd—

November Tuesday 9$^{th}$ this morning got off the Entrance of Tolaga Bay—but the winds baffling us were obliged to warp in with small Anchors & in the Evening Moord with our Best Bower to the Sea in 11 fms Soft Mud. good holding ground

Bearings —Outer part of the Sporings E. B S. End of the Reef off White Island N.N.E. ½ E. Watering place S.E. ½ E.—

{ NB. An Excellent Bay—& well Laid down in Cook's Chart[2]—

All the 10$^{th}$ were Emp$^d$ Wooding and Watering—& the 11$^{th}$ in the Forenoon hove up our Anchors & left the Bay—but the wind coming foul & blowing fresh, put back & anchord in Tolaga Bay again the 12$^{th}$ in the Morning—

here we rode out a gale of Wind from the E.S.E. which threw such a Swell into the Bay that no Boat could get ashore till the 13$^{th}$ at Night—this Time we Anchord with our Best Bower in 7½ fms mudd. & lay with 2 Cables out till the gale abated—

{ Bearings. Outer point of the Sporings E.¼ S. White Is$^d$ NbE¼E. End of the Reef off White Island NE ½ N.

---

[1] Furneaux states that he abandoned his attempt to round Cape Palliser, not because of the danger of a lee shore, but in order 'to compleat our water & wood being in great want of both'. Apart from the need for supplies, the *Adventure's* 'Decks were very leaky, the peoples beds and bedding wet, [and] several of our people complaining of colds . . .'.—*Furneaux's Narrative*, in Beaglehole, *Cook Journals*, II, pp. 741–2.

[2] Cook had called at Tolaga Bay for wood and water in October 1769 on his first voyage.—Beaglehole, *Cook Journals*, I, p. 185.

The Wind continuing at ESE though more Moderate we Staid here till the 16th in which Time we got more Wood & Water on board & put the Ship in tolerable good Order—
Zealanders at Tolaga Bay very friendly—

The Country laid out in plantations—Sweet Potatoes—More Populous, the Land cultivated and the people more Cleanly and Sociable than at Charlotte Sound—

The Girls, how fond of each other

Watering place—behind a high Rock on which is a Hippa or Zealand Fortification—out of Sight and not under protection of the Ship—were very near having a quarrel with the Natives ashore about a Gallon Cagg of Brandy which they stole—& which I had sent for from the Ship for the use of the Wooders & Waterers—

Jack Row would fain have had me seizd one or two of the Zealanders & kept them in our Boat till the Liquor was restored— this I thought dangerous as the Zealanders were too numerous— and all our Empty casks ashore—if Sailors won't take care of their Grogg, they deserve to lose it[1]—

The best chance of getting through Cooks Straits from the Southward is to keep close to the S.W. Shore and if Possible avoid getting to the Eastward of Cape Pallisser—

The N.W. winds we never found to last more than 3 days without interruption and are generally succeeded by a S.W. or Southerly Wind: if it comes to blow hard at N.W. and looks very black it is almost an infallible sign of a sudden shift of wind round to the S.W. & South this we experienced several times when we were unluckily close over to Cape Pallisser or to the Eastward of it or else so far to the Southward as not to get into the Straits before the wind was spent—this Last happend to us but once nor is likely to be often the case as we had Southerly winds for days together, but not keeping the Straits open were unable to profit by them—

had our Ship been able to carry a tolerable Stiff Sail we should nearly have kept our own during a N.W. Wind. This with

---

[1] Jack Row (John Rowe) was the *Adventure's* young master's mate. Burney's view that Rowe's proposed action was dangerous supports Beaglehole's opinion that Rowe was 'overconfident and careless' in dealing with the Maoris. A month later, he was killed in the massacre at Grass Cove (see p. 98).—Beaglehole, *Cook Journals*, II, p. lxxxi.

keeping in to the South Shore would have given us frequent Opportunities—but the Ship was in bad trim and—we not well acquainted with the Coast

The 1st Time we were in Charlotte Sound in the Months of April & May we found very little of the N.W. Winds—the Southerly Winds were then Stronger & more frequent than any other—

Tuesday November 16th at Sunrise left Tolaga Bay but did not get off Cape Pallisser till the 24th having very Squally rough Weather—we kept beating off the Straits Mouth till the 30th when we got a Breeze from the Southward which carried us through, and that Afternoon we Ancord in Ship Cove Charlotte Sound (Novbr 30th)

On coming in we were greatly disappointed at not finding the Resolution here—As soon as the Ship was Secured a Boat was sent to the Watering place—in our garden Stood a Large Tank of Wood on the Top of which was carved LOOK UNDERNEATH— we were not long in obeying the directions & found buried in a Bottle under the Log—a Letter of which the following is a Copy—

> Queen Charlotte Sound New Zealand
> Novbr 24th 1773—
>
> His Britannic Majesty's Sloop, Resolution, Captain Cook— arrived last in this port on the 3d Instt and Saild again on the date hereof. Captn Cook intended to spend a few days in the East Entrance of the Straits looking for the Adventure Captn Furneaux, who he parted company with in the Night of the 29th of last Month— afterwards he will proceed to the South and Eastward—
>
> As Captain Cook has not the least hopes of meeting with Captn Furneaux he will not take upon him to name any place for a Rendezvous. he however thinks of retiring to Easter Island in Latde 27..06 So & Longde 100o..oo' West of Greenwich, about the latter end of next March—it is even probable that he may go to Otaheite or one of the Society Isles; but this will depend so much on Circumstances, that nothing with any degree of certainty can be determined upon—
>
> —James Cook[1]—

---

[1] Unlike the *Adventure*, the *Resolution* had managed to enter Cook Strait soon after the ships were separated. When he arrived at Queen Charlotte Sound on 3 November, Cook was surprised not to find the *Adventure* already there. After waiting in the Sound for three weeks, he decided it was 'hardly possible'

Mem<sup>dms</sup>

Omy present at digging for Capt<sup>n</sup> Cooks Letter—his disbelief & surprize afterwards on finding it—determined to learn to write & began with very good will, but so many people gave him paper, pens etc and set him copies & tasks that in a weeks time the poor fellow's head was bothered—too many Cooks spoilt the Broth—

The Ship Moord in Ship Cove nearly in the Same Birth as before

The next morning (Wednesday December 1<sup>st</sup>) I was sent onshore with the Tent. Waterers, Cooper—one of the Mates (Old Lanyon) the Surgeons Mate & 3 Sick men

Omy ashore with me at the Tent during our Stay here

Dec<sup>r</sup> in the Night it raind very hard—the Tent being old & leaky were obliged to get up & build another Tent within the old one with 2 Steering Sails which we had ashore. luckily we had dug a small ditch round the outside of the Tent which hinderd the water from coming in upon us from the higher grounds—the Rains increasing the River swelld and the run from the Hills was changd into a furious Torrent, that we were obliged to rally forth to secure the Casks from being forced out of the River—they were all full & chockd up with large stones but that not being found security sufficient, we made a Boom of some Branches of Trees and Rope, which we laid across the River, but could not get it ready before 2 casks broke adrift and drove out into the Bay—one of these we found again 2 Days afterwards—

Dec<sup>r</sup> 2<sup>d</sup> The Astronomer erected his Tent close to ours and got his Instruments on shore

found most of our Casks of Bread greatly damaged they having

---

that Furneaux could be 'in any part of New Zealand and I have not heard of him in all this time'. On 25 November he made an unsuccessful search for the *Adventure* along the northern shore of Cook Strait, firing guns every half hour. He finalled concluded that Furneaux had grown tired of attempting to enter Cook Strait and had left for the Cape of Good Hope. On the following day, the two ships only narrowly missed meeting up again. While the *Resolution* was sailing round Cape Palliser from the west, 'fireing guns as usual', the *Adventure* was still trying to round the Cape from the east. With no further rendezvous planned with Furneaux, Cook had 'no expectation of seeing him any more'. He probably also realised that the *Adventure* was unfit for a further voyage to the Antarctic and that it would be preferable to continue his exploration alone.—Beaglehole, *Cook Journals*, II, pp. 286, 297-9.

been buried in the Coals ever since we left England. the Damp has struck through the Casks (New Butt Ironbound)—were obliged to throw a great deal away and to get the rest on Shore with our oven to bake over again—

imagine the Resolutions Bread must have been in the same condition for we see their oven has been set up and a good deal of bread dust lying by the place—

The Zealanders come down to the Ship every day

Emp.d overhauling and repairing the Rigging and Sail. Wooding, Watering &c and getting ready for Sea as fast as possible.

find nothing of the Hogs we left here, not so much as the least traces of them[1]—

Fowls left here by Capt.n Cook grown very shy & in a fair way of having a fine breed—Saw 10 Eggs a good way up in the woods under a hollow Tree—Omy says he saw a Hen with 3 young ones in his Rambles—The Fowls on being disturbed have taken a flight of above 100 yards without alighting—

Pease—run wild—believe the Resolution have had a good share of them—

Saturday December 11.th finish baking the Bread & got it all on board much mended—a great deal very bad yet—

Sunday 12.th Dec.r in Shag Cove.—Kemp, Rowe, Omy & myself in the Great Cutter—Narrow Escape there[2]—

Tuesday December 14.th in the Night some Indians by the Negligence of the Centinel, got to the Tent and took every thing they could lay their hands on and carried to a small canoe that lay hid among the Rocks:—2 Musquets, a Cutlass—Several Bags of Linnen & many other things but being too greedy they were at last discovered after having made several successfull trips and almost compleated their Cargo—Mr Baily[3] the Astronomer who first discovered the Thieves, fired at one of them with small shot but they Escaped to the woods—the next morning we saw some drops

---

[1] See p. 56 and p. 56 n. 1.
[2] Now Resolution Bay. Neither Burney nor Arthur Kempe, the *Adventure's* First Lieutenant, elaborated on the incident in their official writings.— A. Kempe, *Log* and *Journal*, PRO Adm. 51/4520; J. Burney, *Log* and *Journal*, PRO Adm. 51/4523.
[3] William Bayly.

of Blood along the Beach from which I supose M.<sup>r</sup> Bailys shot were not thrown away—we found the Canoe well loaded and every thing that was missing except a Shirt and Blanket—this is not their first attempt

One Night last week they came with 3 Canoes full of men, but luckily we had been alarmd just before and were on our guard on which they thought proper to retire—we constantly in the Night, kept a fire without the Tent at the Distance of about 10 yards, for the benefit of the Centinel—the Night that the Zealanders made their first attempt & which I believe was with an intention, had they caught us all napping, to have knockd out our Brains—The Centinel had come within the Tent to get Some Tobacco and left his Arms by the Fire—on coming out he saw an Indian standing by the Fire on which he immediately calld out & gave the Alarm—but was afraid to go for his Arms—we all got up & lookd about us but not seeing any Canoe near the Beach or any other Signs of a Stranger having been near us I concluded the Centinel had been dreaming—however we all lay down with our Cloaths on and our Arms by us—and about an hour after had notice of the 3 Canoes—on their coming within a Ships length o the beach, I ordered one of the People to Fire a Musquet over their heads, on which they halted, and after a consultation, amongst themselves of at least 5 minutes—went away. fear of the Ship which lay about 3/4 of a mile from the Beach, hindered them, I believe more than their dread of us, from prosecuting their enterprise—though we should have been able to have puzzled them a little for besides what we could have killd in the landing— we could after have taken to the Tent and by favour of the darkness of the Night have defended it long enough to sicken them—

The 2.<sup>d</sup> attempt there was but one small Canoe & I believe only 3 men—

Dec. 16<sup>th</sup> Thursday The Astronomer struck his Tent and went on board with his instruments—

Friday 17<sup>th</sup>. M.<sup>r</sup> Rowe was sent up the Sound for Greens with Orders not to stay later than 3 in the afternoon at farthest as we proposed sailing next morning—

This not the first time our Boat has been up the Sound by a great many nor would it now be thought worthy remark but on account of what followed—

This morning some Indians came to the Tent and had the Impudence to ask for their Canoe—which however, as we were on the eve of sailing I let them have—before noon we Struck the Tent and got every thing on board—in the Afternoon hoisted the Launch in—and only waited for the Cutter, to Unmoor—

Saturday 18ᵗʰ. The Cutter not returning we began to imagine some accident had happened—accordingly the Launch was hoisted out and sent Mannd & Armed to search after her—an hour before Midnight the Launch returned with the melancholy Account of the Cutter & her Crew being cutt off by the Natives— by which dreadfull Accident we lost a good Officer & many of our best Seamen[1]—

Sunday 19ᵗʰ at Daylight unmoord and got under sail but the wind dying away Anchord again between Ship Cove and the Motuara Island

Monday 20ᵗʰ at 4 in the Morning got under sail, but the wind failing again were obliged to anchor nearly in the same place— at Night the wind blew Strong from the N.W. and next day we had a hard Gale of Wind with most violent Squalls from every Quarter, owing to the irregularity of the Land about us the True Wind being at N.W. we were obliged to weather this Gale out at Single Anchor the Ship turning round every minute would have made it impossible for us to have kept a Clear Hawse— luckly the Squalls were Short lived & succeded one another so

---

[1] Burney's report to Furneaux on the massacre of ten of the *Adventure's* men at Grass Cove (now Whareunga Bay) is printed in the Appendix. In his private journal, Burney does not even mention that he was the officer in charge of the expedition which found the men's remains. Shocked by the scene he had witnessed, he no doubt felt the details were far too gruesome for his family and friends. Even when Burney arrived back in England over seven months later, he would mention the affair only 'in a whisper'. It was not until Cook returned to Queen Charlotte Sound in February 1777 that he was able to ascertain the details of the massacre, which had been the culmination of increasing hostility between the Maoris and the Europeans. While the ten men were having lunch at Grass Cove they had a quarrel with some Maoris, probably over the theft of food. The Europeans fired two muskets and killed two Maoris, whereupon the others attacked and killed all the white men. The bodies were immediately cooked and eaten. Like Burney, Cook considered that the massacre was not premeditated on the part of the Maoris and that the Europeans' impulsive behaviour was probably partly to blame.—Ellis, *Early Diary of Frances Burney*, Vol. II, p. 283; Beaglehole, *Cook Journals*, III, pp. 63–4.

quick that our Cable had not Time to tighten, otherways it could not have withstood the force of the wind so as to have brought the Ship round up in the middle of a Squall. towards the Evening the wind blew more regular—

Wednesd. 22ᵈ in the Afternoon we hove our Anchor up & came to sail with a Modᵗ Breeze at N.W.—we ran round the Hippa and at ½ past 3 got out of Charlotte Sound & stood through Cooks Straits Next morning took our Departure from C. Pallisser it bearing N. 3/4 E. distance 13 or 14 Leagues which was the last we saw of the Land[1]—

---

[1] Burney did not continue his journal-letter after the *Adventure's* departure from New Zealand. Furneaux intended to sail again to the Antarctic but, when he reached 56°S, the high seas and intense cold led him to change his course for Cape Horn. By the time he approached the Cape, he was short of supplies, his men were falling ill and he realised that the *Adventure* was in no condition for further Antarctic exploration. Before heading for England, he made another unsuccessful search for Bouvet's Cape Circumcision in the South Atlantic. On 19 March 1774 the *Adventure* arrived at the Cape of Good Hope to refit and a month later left for England, anchoring off Spithead on 14 July. The *Resolution* did not arrive back in England until over a year later on 30 July 1775, after making two further voyages to the Antarctic and one to the Pacific Islands.

# APPENDIX

## The Grass Cove Massacre[1]

Saturday December 18th 1773. This morning, I was orderd in the Launch (she being well man'd & armd) to go in quest of the Cutter. My instructions were first to look well into East Bay & then proceed to Grass Cove (the place where Mr Rowe was order'd) & if I heard nothing of the Boat there to go further up the Sound & come down along the West Shore. As Mr Rowe had left the Ship an hour earlier than the time proposed, & in a great hurry, I was strongly perswaded his Curiosity had carried him into East Bay, none in our Ship having ever been there before, or else Some accident had happen'd to the Boat; either gone adrift through the Boatkeepers Negligence, or been stove among the Rocks—this was almost every body's opinion, & on this Suposition the Carpenters Mate was sent with me with some sheets of Tin. I had not the least suspicion of their having receivd any injury from the Natives, our boats having frequently been higher up & worse provided. About 10 we left the Ship—having a light breeze in our favour we soon got round Long Island & within Long Point. I rounded every Cove on the Larboard Hand as we went along, looking well all round with a Spy Glass which I took for that purpose—at ½ past 1 We Stoppd at a beach on the left hand side going up East Bay, to boil some Victuals, as we brought nothing with us but raw meat—while we were cooking I saw an Indian on the Opposite Shore running along a beach up towards the head of the Bay. Our Victuals being drest, we got it in the boat & put off—& in a Short time got to the head of this

[1] J. Burney, *Log*, PRO Adm. 51/4523.

Reach where we saw an Indian Settlement—as we drew near Some of the Indians came down on the Rocks & waved for us to begone, but seeing we disregarded them, they alterd their Notes—here we found 6 large Canoes hauld up on the Beach—most of them double ones—a great many people but not so many as one might expect from the Number of houses & Size of the Canoes. leaving the Boats Crew to guard the Boat, I stept on shore with the Marines (the Corporal & 5 men) & searchd a good many of their houses, but found nothing to give me any Suspicion—3 or 4 well beaten paths led further into the Woods, where were many more houses—but the people continuing very friendly I thought it unnecessary to continue our search—coming down to the Boat, one of the Indians had brought a bundle of Hepatoos (long Spears) down to the beach—but seeing I lookd very earnestly at him, he put them on the ground & walkd about with seeming unconcern. Some of the people appearing to be frightend I gave a Looking Glass to one & a large Nail to another—from this place the Bay ran nearly as I could guess NNW a good mile where it Ended in a long sandy beach—I lookd all round with the glass but saw no boat, Canoe or Sign of Inhabitants—I therefore contented myself with firing some Guns which I did in every Cove as I went along. I now kept close to the East Shore & came to another Settlement where the Indians invited us ashore. I enquired of them about the Boat, to which they pretended ignorance—they appeard very friendly here & sold us some fish—within an hour we left this place, in a small beach adjoining to Grass Cove we saw a very large double canoe just hauld up, with 2 men & a Dog—the men on seeing us left their Canoe & ran up into the woods—this gave me reason to Suspect I should here get some tidings of our Cutter—we went ashore & Searchd the Canoe where we found one of the Rullock ports of the Cutter & some Shoes one of which was known to belong to M$^r$ Woodhouse, one of our Midshipmen, who went with M$^r$ Rowe—one of the people at the same time brought me a piece of meat, which he took to be some of the Salt Meat belonging to the Cutter's Crew—on examining this & smelling to it I found it was fresh meat—M$^r$ Fannin, (the Master) who was with me, supos'd it was Dog's flesh & I was of the same opinion, for I still doubted their being Cannibals: but we were Soon convinced by most horrid & undeniable proofs—a great many baskets (about 20) laying on the beach tied up, we cut them open, some were full of roasted flesh

& some of fern root which serves them for bread—on further
search we found more shoes & a hand which we immediately
knew to have belong'd to Tho^s Hill one of our Forecastlemen, it
being marked T.H. which he had got done at Otaheite with a
tattow instrument—I went with some of the people a little way
up the woods, but saw nothing else—coming down again was a
round spot cover'd with fresh earth, about 4 feet diameter, where
Something had been buried: having no spade we began to dig
with a Cutlass—in the mean time I launchd the Canoe with an
intention to destroy her—but seeing a great smoke ascending
over the nearest hill, I got all the people in the boat & made what
haste I could to be with them before Sunsett—on opening the
next bay, which was Grass Cove, we saw 4 Canoes—a Single, &
3 double ones—a great many People on the beach—a large fire
was on the top of the High Land beyond the woods, frome whence
all the way down the Hill the place was throngd like a Fair—
those who were near the Shore had retreated to a small hill within
a Ships length of the water side, where they stood talking to us—
as we came in I order'd a Musquetoon to be fired through one of
the Canoes, as we suspected they might be full of men laying down
in the bottom, but nobody was in them—the Savages on the
little hill still kept hollowing & making Signs for us to come ashore
—however as soon as we had got close in we all fired—the first
Volley did not seem to affect them much—.but on the 2^d they
began to scramble away as fast as they could, some of them
howling—we continued firing as long as we could see the least
glimpse of a man through the bushes—amongst the Indians
were 2 very stout men who never offer'd to move till they found
themselves forsaken by their companions & then they walkd away
with great composure & deliberation—their pride not Suffering
them to run—one of them however stumbled, & just made Shift
to crawl off on all fours—the other got clear without any apparent
hurt—I then landed with the Marines & left M^r Fannin to guard
the boat—on the beach were 2 bundles of Cellery which had been
gather'd for loading the Cutter—a plain proof that the attack
was made here—a broken piece of an Oar was stuck upright in
the Ground to which they had tied their Canoes—I then searchd all
along at the back of the beach to see if the Cutter was there—we
found no boat—but instead of her—Such a shocking scene of
Carnage & Barbarity as can never be mentiond or thought of,
but with horror.—whilst we remained almost stupified on this

spot M$^r$ Fannin call'd to us that he heard the Savages gathering together in the Valley, on which I returned to the Boat & hauld alongside the Canoes, 3 of which we demolished—whilst this was transacting, the fire on the top of the High Land disappeard & the Indians had gatherd together in the wood, where we heard them at very high words, doubtless quarelling whether or no they should come to attack us & try to save their Canoes—it now grew dark. I therefore just stept out & lookd once more along the back of the beach to see if the Cutter had been hauld up in the bushes—but seeing nothing of her returned & put off—our whole force would have been but barely sufficient to have gone up the Hill, & to have ventured with half (for one half must have been left to guard the Boat) would have been madness—As we open'd the upper part of the Sound we saw a very large fire about 3 or 4 miles higher up—this fire formd a complete Oval, reaching from the top of a hill down to the water Side—the middle space being inclosed all round by the fire, like a hedge—I consulted with M$^r$ Fannin & we were both of Opinion that we could expect to reap no other advantage than the poor Satisfaction of killing some of the Savages—at leaving Grass Cove we had fired a general Volley towards where we heard the Indians talking—but by going in & out of the boat the Arms had got wet & some 4 of the pieces mist fire—what was still worse it began to rain—our ammunition was more than half expended & we left 6 Large Canoes behind us in one place—I therefore did not think it worth while to proceed where nothing could be hoped for but revenge.

Coming between 2 round Islands that lay to the Southward of East Bay we imagined we heard somebody calling—we lay on our Oars & listened but heard no more of it—we hollowd several times but to little purpose the poor Souls were far enough out of hearing—& indeed I think it some comfort to reflect that in all probability every man of them must have been killd on the Spot. We got on board between 11 & 12—

The people lost in the Cutter wer M$^r$ Rowe, M$^r$ Woodhouse, Francis Murphy Quartermaster, W$^m$ Facey. Tho$^s$ Hill. Edw$^d$ Jones, Michael Bell, Jn$^o$ Cavenaugh Tho$^s$ Milton & James Swilley the Capt$^{ns}$ Man—4 of them belongd to the Forecastle & 2 to the After guard—being 10 in all—most of these were of our very best Seamen—the Stoutest & most healthy people in the Ship—We brought on board 2 Hands—one belonging to Mr

Rowe, known by a hurt he had received in it the other to Thomas Hill as beforementiond, & the head of the Capt$^{ns}$ Servant—these with more of the remains were tied in a Hammock & thrown overboard with ballast & Shot sufficient to sink it—we found none of their Arms or Cloaths except part of a pair of Trowsers, a Frock & 6 shoes—no 2 of them being fellows—

I am not inclined to think this was any premeditated plan of these Savages, as the morning M$^r$ Rowe left the Ship he met 2 Canoes who came down & staid all the forenoon in Ship Cove. It might probably happen from Some quarrel, or the fairness of the Opportunity tempted them; our people being so very incautious & thinking themselves to Secure—another thing which encouraged the Zealanders was, they were sensible a Gun was not infallible. that they sometimes mist & that when discharged they must be loaded again, which time they knew how to take advantage of. after their Success I imagine was a general meeting on the East Side of the Sound—the Indians of Shag Cove were there— this we knew by a Cock which was in one of the Canoes, & by a long Single Canoe which I had seen 4 days before in Shag Cove where I had been with M$^r$ Rowe in the Cutter.

# BIBLIOGRAPHY

## A. WORKS BY JAMES BURNEY

### i. PUBLISHED

*Plan of Defence against Invasion*, London, 1797.

*Measures Recommended for the Support of Public Credit*, London, 1797.

*A Chronological History of the Discoveries in the South Sea or Pacific Ocean*, 5 vols., London, 1803–17.

*Observations on the Progress of Bodies Floating in a Stream*, London, 1808.

*New Method Proposed for Measuring a Ship's Rate of Sailing*, London, 1808.

*Memoir, explanatory of a Chart, of the Coast of China, and the Sea Eastward, from the River of Canton, to the Southern Islands of Japan*, London, 1811. (Reprinted in 1813 as appendix to Volume III of *A Chronological History of the Discoveries in the South Sea or Pacific Ocean*.)

*History of the Buccaneers of America*, London, 1816. (Reprinted from Volume IV of *A Chronoligical History of the Discoveries in the South Sea or Pacific Ocean*.)

*A Memoir on the Geography of the North-Eastern Part of Asia, and on the question whether Asia and America are contiguous, or are separated by the sea*, London, 1818.

*A Chronological History of North-Eastern Voyages of Discovery; and of the early Eastern navigations of the Russians*, London, 1819.

*A Commentary on the Systems which have been advanced for explaining the Planetary Motions*, London, 1819.

*A Memoir on the Voyage of d'Entrecasteaux, in search of La Pérouse*, London, 1820.

*An Essay, by way of Lecture, on the Game of Whist*, London, 1821. (Posthumous editions appeared in 1823 as *A Treatise on the Game of Whist* and in 1842 as *A Concise Treatise on the Game of Whist*.)

101

ii.  UNPUBLISHED LOGS AND JOURNALS OF COOK'S SECOND AND
      THIRD VOYAGES

*Second voyage:*  Log.  18 November 1772–23 January 1774.
                         (Includes details of Grass Cove
                         massacre.) PRO Adm.51/4523.

                  Journal.  19 November 1772–20 May 1774.
                            PRO Adm.51/4523.

*Third voyage:*  Journal.  10 February 1776–26 April 1778.
                           PRO Adm.51/4528.

                 Journal.  10 February 1776–24 August 1779.
                           MS. in Mitchell Library
                           (Includes report of Cook's death.)

## B.  WORKS ON THE BURNEY FAMILY

Arblay, Madame d', *Memoirs of Doctor Burney*, 3 vols., London, 1832.

Articles on Dr. Charles Burney, Dr. Charles Burney (Jnr.), Frances
    Burney (Madame d'Arblay), James Burney and Sarah Harriet
    Burney in *Dictionary of National Biography*, London, 1886, Vols.
    II and VII.

Barrett, Charlotte (ed.), *Diary and Letters of Madame d'Arblay*, 1778–1840.
    6 vols., London, 1904.

Ellis, Annie Raine (ed.), *The Early Diary of Frances Burney 1768–1778*,
    2 vols., London, 1907.

Hemlow, Joyce, *The History of Fanny Burney*, Oxford, 1958.

Johnson, R. Brimley, *Fanny Burney and the Burneys*, London, 1926.

Manwaring, G.E., *My Friend the Admiral. The Life, Letters, and Journals
    of Rear-Admiral James Burney, F.R.S. The Companion of Captain Cook
    and Friend of Charles Lamb*, London, 1931.

Scholes, Percy, *The Great Doctor Burney*, 2 vols., London, 1948.

## C.  VOYAGES

### i.  PUBLISHED

Beaglehole, J.C. (ed.), *The Endeavour Journal of Joseph Banks, 1768–1771*,
    2 vols., Sydney, 1962.

————*The Journals of Captain James Cook on his Voyages of Discovery*,
    4 vols. and Portfolio, Cambridge, 1955–67.

Bligh, William, *A Voyage to the South Sea in H.M.S. Bounty, including an
    account of the mutiny on board the said ship*, London, 1792.

Boosé, Jas. A. (ed.), *Crozet's Voyage to Tasmania, New Zealand, the
    Ladrone Islands, and the Philippines in the Years 1771–1772*, trans.
    H. Ling Roth, London, 1891.

Bougainville, Lewis de, *A Voyage Round the World*, trans. J.R. Forster, London, 1772.

Carrington, Hugh (ed.), *The Discovery of Tahiti. A Journal of the Second Voyage of H.M.S. Dolphin . . . written by her master, George Robertson*, London, 1948.

Forster, Johann Georg Adam, *A Voyage Round the World, in His Britannic Majesty's Sloop, Resolution, Commanded by Capt. James Cook, During the Years 1772, 3, 4 and 5*, 2 vols., London, 1777.

Kerguelen, M. de, *Relation de Deux Voyages dans les Mers Australes & des Indies, faits en 1771, 1772, 1773 & 1774*, Paris, 1782.

Markham, Clements (ed.), *The Voyages of Pedro Fernandez de Quiros, 1595 to 1606*, London, 1944.

Rutter, Owen (ed.), *Anders Sparrman. A Voyage round the World with Captain James Cook in H.M.S. Resolution*, trans. Huldine Beamish and Averil Mackenzie-Grieve, London, 1953.

Sharp, Andrew, *The Voyages of Abel Janszoon Tasman*, Oxford, 1968.

## ii.  UNPUBLISHED

*Cook's second voyage*

Logs and journals of several persons who sailed on Cook's second voyage are in the Public Record Office, Admiralty Series 51 and 55. These include:

*Resolution*

| | |
|---|---|
| R. Cooper, First Lieutenant | PRO Adm.55/104, 109 |
| C. Clerke, Second Lieutenant | 55/103 |
| R. Pickersgill, Third Lieutenant | 51/4553 |

(See also National Maritime Museum, Greenwich, 57/038.)

*Adventure*

| | |
|---|---|
| T. Furneaux, Commander | 55/1 |

(See also B.M. Add. MS 27890.)

| | |
|---|---|
| A. Kempe, Second Lieutenant, later First Lieutenant | 55/4520 |
| R. Hergest, Midshipman | 51/4522 |

For a complete list of logs and journals written on Cook's second voyage, see Beaglehole, *The Journals of Captain James Cook on his Voyages of Discovery*, II, pp. cxv–clvii.

*Other voyages*

| | |
|---|---|
| S. Wallis, *Dolphin Log* | PRO Adm. 55/35. |

## D. BOOKS, PAMPHLETS AND ARTICLES

Adams, Henry, *Memoirs of Arii Taimai*, Paris, 1901.

Ainger, A. (ed.), *The Letters of Charles Lamb*, 2 vols., London, 1904.

Beaglehole, J.C., *The Death of Captain Cook*, Canberra, 1964.

———*The Exploration of the Pacific*, third ed., London, 1966.

Best, Elsdon, *The Maori*, 2 vols., Wellington, 1924.

Buck, Peter, *The Coming of the Maori*, second ed., Wellington, 1950.

Chapman, R.W. (ed.), *The Letters of Samuel Johnson*, 3 vols., Oxford, 1952.

Clark, T.B., *Omai, First Polynesian Ambassador to England*, San Francisco, 1941.

Cockayne, Leonard, *The Vegetation of New Zealand*, third ed., Weinheim/Bergstr., 1958.

Cornwall, Barry, *Charles Lamb: A Memoir*, London, 1869.

Day, A. Grove and Stroven, Carl (ed.), *A Hawaiian Reader*, New York, 1959.

Furneaux, Rupert, *Tobias Furneaux*, London, 1960.

Gunson, Niel, 'A Note on the Difficulties of Ethnohistorical Writing, with Special Reference to Tahiti', *Journal of the Polynesian Society*, 72 (1963), pp. 415–19.

Handy, E.S. Craighill, *History and Culture in the Society Islands*, Bernice P. Bishop Museum Bulletin 79, Honolulu, 1930.

———*Polynesian Religion*, Bernice P. Bishop Museum Bulletin 34, Honolulu, 1927.

Henry, Teuira, *Ancient Tahiti*, Bernice P. Bishop Museum Bulletin 48, Honolulu, 1928.

Keith, H.H. (ed.), *The Queeney Letters*, London, 1934.

Lamb, Charles, *The Essays of Elia*, London, 1883.

Langdon, Robert, 'A View on Ari'i Taimai's Memoirs', *Journal of Pacific History*, 4 (1969), pp. 162–5.

Lewis, M.A., *England's Sea-Officers*, London, 1939.

Lloyd, Christopher and Anderson, R.C. (ed.), *A Memoir of James Trevenen*, London, 1959.

Lloyd, Christopher and Coulter, Jack L.S., *Medicine and the Navy 1200–1900. III. 1714–1815*, London, 1961.

Marcus, G.J., *A Naval History of England. I. The Formative Centuries*, London, 1961.

Mead, S.M., *Traditional Maori Clothing*, Wellington, 1969.

*Omiah's Farewell: Inscribed to the Ladies of London*, London, 1776.

Phipps, C.J., *A Voyage Towards the North Pole*, London, 1774.

Rietz, Rolf du, 'Three Letters from James Burney to Sir Joseph Banks. A contribution to the History of William Bligh's "A Voyage to the South Sea" ', *Ethnos*, 27 (1962), pp. 115–25.

Roth, H. Ling, *The Aborigines of Tasmania*, second ed., Halifax, 1899.

Sadler, Thomas (ed.), *Diary, Reminiscences, and Correspondence of Henry Crabb Robinson*, 3 vols., London, 1869.

Samwell, David, *Narrative of the Death of Captain James Cook*, London, 1786.

Shawcross, Wilfred, 'The Cambridge University Collection of Maori Artefacts, made on Captain Cook's First Voyage', *Journal of the Polynesian Society*, 79 (1970), pp. 312–20.

Turberville, A.S. (ed.), *Johnson's England. An account of the Life & Manners of his Age*, 2 vols., Oxford, 1933.

Waller, A.R. and Glover, Arnold (ed.), *The Collected Works of William Hazlitt*, 13 vols., London, 1902–6.

Williamson, R.W., *The Social and Political Systems of Central Polynesia*, 3 vols., Cambridge, 1924.

# INDEX